574.5   Blashfield, Jean F.
BLA   Endangered species.

                         33197000037866

$26.60

DATE		
9-5		

DISCARDED

BAKER & TAYLOR BOOKS

Endangered

Species

ENDANGERED SPECIES

Jean F. Blashfield

Educational Consultant
Helen J. Challand, Ph.D.
Professor of Science Education, National-Louis University

Technical Consultant
Alice Clarke
Editor, *Endangered Species UPDATE*
University of Michigan

CHILDRENS PRESS®
CHICAGO

A production of B&B Publishing, Inc.

Project Editor: Jean Blashfield Black   **Artist:** Diane Hamil
Editor: Marjorie Benson   **Production Manager:** Dave Conant
Designer: Elizabeth B. Graf   **Photo Researcher:** Terri Willis
Cover Design: Margrit Fiddle

Printed on Evergreen Gloss
50% recycled preconsumer waste
Binder's board made from 100% recycled material

Library of Congress Cataloging-in-Publication Data

Blashfield, Jean F.
    Endangered species / Jean F. Blashfield and Wallace B. Black.
        p.   cm. — (Saving planet earth)
    Includes index.
    Summary: Identifies and tells the stories behind many plants and animals at
risk from human action, and describes the political and other factors involved in
decisions concerning the various species.
    ISBN 0-516-05514-3
    1. Endangered species—Juvenile literature. 2. Endangered plants—Juvenile
literature. 3. Man—Influence on nature—Juvenile literature. [1. Rare animals.
2. Rare plants. 3. Man—Influence on nature.] I. Black, Wallace B. II. Title.
III. Series.
    QH75.B57   1992
    574.5'29—dc20

                                         92-9083
                                          CIP
                                          AC

Cover photo—© Imtek Imagineering/Masterfile

TABLE OF CONTENTS

Chapter 1

Hawaii—Laboratory
for Extinction

THE LARGE DOUBLE-HULLED CANOES pulled onto a sandy beach. The men and women climbed out, alert for any indication of danger. But the beach that seemed to go on forever remained empty of threat.

The explorers from islands far away had been traveling for many weeks across the vast and apparently endless ocean. They were certain they would arrive somewhere, but little did these travelers from the Marquesas Islands in the South Pacific dream that they would arrive at an untouched paradise of many islands. Dense forest covered the main islands. Spectacular waterfalls dropped thousands of feet into green valleys. The air was filled with the scent of flowers and the songs and flashing colors of birds.

As the newcomers traveled through the long chain of volcanic islands called an archipelago, each new step brought a new and unexpected sight of the natural riches.

The year was about A.D. 400. The islands the Polynesian explorers arrived at were the Hawaiian Islands—or, as Captain Cook called them in 1778, the Sandwich Islands.

Until the brave explorers from the Marquesas arrived, there had been no human life on the islands. Hawaii was farther from a continent than any other land on Earth. Even so, there had been other kinds of colonists. Birds, insects, and plant seeds arrived to settle there, blown in on the winds or floating across the sea as the islands were built up by lava flows from undersea volcanoes over many thousands of years. These living things

The Hawaiian Islands were formed by lava flowing from the tops of ancient volcanoes. Mauna Loa and Kilauea on the island of Hawaii are still active.

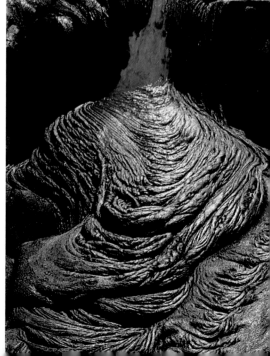

eventually changed, or evolved, into types of plants and animals that are *endemic* to Hawaii—they don't exist anywhere else on Earth. Naturalists looking back at that ancient paradise think that as many as 95 percent of all Hawaiian plants, birds, and mollusks lived nowhere else. The only mammals were a species of monk seal and a hoary bat. A finchlike bird that arrived in the islands—possibly from North America—gradually evolved into 23 different species of a family of birds called honeycreepers.

These endemic plants and animals developed in isolation, and they could not survive when that isolation was broken.

The newest colonists, human beings, started their work by clearing the forest. In the clearings they planted bananas and other plants they brought from their native islands. Decade by decade, the Polynesians multiplied and settled more land.

Early immigrants from Tahiti introduced goats to Hawaii. These animals eagerly ate the native vegetation and altered the habitat for many other animals.

Then came an even greater shock. About a thousand years ago, a second great wave of human colonists began to arrive, this time from Tahiti. They brought new crop plants such as sugarcane and coconuts. Even more important, however, they brought mammals—dogs and rats and pigs and goats that quickly claimed the land as theirs. The native plants and animals had never before had to defend themselves against such creatures.

The early settlers must have been wide-eyed at the huge numbers of colorful birds. The uniqueness of these birds eventually caused their disappearance. As the tribal people set up new traditions on the islands, the birds' colorful feathers played an important role, especially in costumes for royalty. One magnificent cape required the feathers of 80,000 birds. Leis, the colorful good-luck necklaces now made of flowers, were originally made of feathers.

A number of the Hawaiian birds were flightless birds whose relatives elsewhere could fly. One species of goose stood at least 3 feet (1 meter) high. These birds had no defenses when human invaders introduced mammals. And the people dined on the birds' succulent meat.

FACT

Scientists from the National Museum of Natural History have found the bones of 32 types of extinct Hawaiian birds. Usually the remains of extinct animals are fossils from millions of years ago. But these birds were alive just 1,600 years ago. Their disappearance can be blamed directly on humans.

Europeans Reach the Islands. By the late 1700s when people from Europe began to reach the islands, the Hawaiian people had wiped out almost 50 bird species. Even so, when Captain Cook arrived, there were still about 70 different species of birds on Hawaii. Of those, 23 are now extinct, and 30 are in danger of dying out.

By 1853 Hawaiian officials were noting that some species

of birds might need to be protected. However, nothing was done. In fact, newcomers continued to introduce new species to the islands.

On Laysan at the far end of the archipelago, rabbits introduced by Europeans destroyed so much vegetation within a few years that three birds—the Laysan rail, the Laysan millerbird, and the Laysan honeycreeper—became extinct. When rats were introduced on nearby Midway island, three more bird species were added to the extinct list.

A scientist at Hawaii's Bishop Museum estimated that the human invasion of the islands had brought in about 2,000 insects and other arthropods, 900 plant species, 50 species of birds, and 18 mammals. And it doesn't stop—each year at least 20 new species of insects are introduced into Hawaii.

FACT

Settlers from the United States and Europe brought their own species with them so that they wouldn't feel so far from home. Numerous delicate plants that had to be grown indoors in northern countries took root in the tropical islands and stole habitat from the native plants. When you think about Hawaii, the greenery in your mind's eye was probably introduced.

There are more endangered species on the Hawaiian islands alone than in all of North America. *Endangered* species are on the

The bluestripe snapper was brought to Hawaii about 35 years ago. Its population is increasing at the expense of the native fish species.

verge of extinction and will probably not survive unless humans take drastic action to save them. *Threatened* species will probably become endangered unless their habitat—the natural setting in which they thrive—is protected.

The first national law identifying and protecting endangered species in the United States was passed in 1966. In the first listing of species to be protected by the law, 36 species of birds were listed as threatened or endangered, including 20 native to Hawaii. Today, eight more have been added to the list.

The damage to Hawaii's native plants and animals still goes on. The state draws tourists from all over the world. The population is growing, and the original species are being pushed farther and farther up the mountainsides. Many of them cannot live in such settings.

FACT

Brown tree snakes were taken to Guam from the nearby Solomon Islands during World War II (1939-1945). On Guam, the burgeoning snake population ate three species of birds into extinction. Today, with fewer birds to eat them, the expanding insect population is devastating the plant population of Guam. Brown tree snakes have now been introduced into Hawaii, probably by tourists. Think about what can happen.

The Palila

The palila is a member of the Hawaiian honeycreeper family. This songbird's population consists of only a little more than 1,000 birds living on the slopes of Mauna Kea. It depends completely on a yellow-flowered evergreen called

the mamane tree. The palila feeds on its seeds, builds nests in it, and munches on an insect that lives in it. Obviously, the mamane must be protected if the birds are to survive. But wild sheep and goats living on the mountain are destroying the mamane, especially growing seedlings.

The palila depends entirely on the mamane tree for its food and for nesting. Protecting this tree from sheep and goats living on Mauna Kea's slopes will help its small population survive.

Everyone was in favor of getting rid of the sheep and goats except hunters, who had come to regard them as their legitimate targets. The federal government wanted to take care of the palila and its habitat, but the state was more interested in pleasing the hunters. The Sierra Club Legal Defense Fund entered a lawsuit in the name of the bird itself, claiming that the state, by allowing the ecosystem to become further degraded, was, in fact, going against the Endangered Species Act. The palila won. The forest of mamane trees is expanding again. For the moment, at least, the palila birds seem secure.

Permanent residents and visitors to Hawaii need to be aware of the damage humans can cause. New housing developments (right) *and garbage strewn on beaches* (left) *both cause problems for wildlife.*

But Isn't Hawaii a Special Case?

Yes and no.

It's special in that the extinctions on Hawaii took place over such a brief period of time and clearly result from the activities of humans.

But the same thing is happening all over the planet in less clearly defined ways. Many species of plants and animals are becoming extinct due to the assault on their natural habitats by the huge and growing human population.

Every plant or animal in danger of extinction has its own dramatic story. There are too many to tell. A few stories will be told in the following pages. Multiply them by the hundreds to get the true picture.

Currently, there are more than 1,130 species on the official United States list of endangered species, which includes many from other countries. Unfortunately, thousands more are waiting to become official. Before anyone puts them on the list so that rescue efforts can begin many of those will become extinct.

Only by people caring about other living things, and fighting to keep them safe, will extinction be prevented for many plants and animals. Biologist Edward O. Wilson of Harvard University calls species loss "the folly our descendants are least likely to forgive."

The Trumpeter Swan

The exploration of new lands by Europeans often brought the discovery of species with a commercial value. Over and over again, businessmen have driven the species they depend on for their living to the edge of extinction.

When explorers first ventured into the interior of North America, they marveled at the beautiful white trumpeter swan. There were sometimes so many in a flock that they turned the earth white as far as a person could see.

Trumpeter swans are the largest waterfowl in the world. Males (cobs) may be more than 5 feet (1.5 meters) long, have a wingspan of 8 feet (2.4 meters), and weigh 36 pounds (16 kilograms). The females (pens) lay three to five eggs each year. Trumpeters mate for life. They feed by tipping up in the water and reaching for aquatic plants with their long necks. Their loud trumpeting call echoes across the countryside when they migrate, their long necks stretched out. A trumpeter swan has an all-black beak. The similar mute swan, introduced from Europe as an ornamental bird, has an orange beak and is, of course, silent. Mute swans have taken over trumpeter habitats.

Trumpeter swans were killed in huge numbers because their long feathers made excellent quill pens for writing.

Soon after trumpeter swans were discovered in the New World, people found that long feathers called quills held ink and made excellent pens. Trumpeter swan quills were by far the best, and the easiest way to get them was by killing the bird.

By 1932, the number of trumpeters known to exist was down to fewer than 70 birds hidden away in the mountains of Montana. (Several trumpeter colonies were later found in remote parts of Canada and Alaska.) Concerned naturalists in Canada and the United States began to protect and breed the birds. Red Rock Lakes National Wildlife Refuge in Montana was created in 1935 to help protect the birds. Years later, however, it became clear that the protected wild populations might not survive. Naturalists began breeding the birds in captivity and then releasing them into the wild.

But a strange thing happened. Many birds bred in captivity and returned to the wild lost their instinct to migrate somewhere along the line. Only those few birds raised in the wild still know how to migrate from Canada back to Chesapeake Bay where the birds traditionally wintered.

Bill Lishman, a sculptor and pilot from Blackstock in Ontario, Canada, is trying to teach them to migrate.

Lishman started by training Canada geese (more easily obtained than swans) to fly beside him when he ran, while playing a tape recording of the engine of a very small, light-

Trumpeter swan nests in the wetlands of Minto Flats, Alaska, are carefully monitored by biologists to ensure the survival of the young cygnets when they hatch.

16

Biologists band a trumpeter swan for identification purposes prior to releasing it into the wild. The band allows researchers to find out where the swan goes.

weight airplane called an ultralight. Then he succeeded in getting the geese to follow him into the air, flying in formation along with his ultralight, ignoring the noise and fumes.

Lishman is now trying to transfer his technique to trumpeter swans. If they will fly along with him, he'll show the Canadian birds the way to Chesapeake Bay.

Other naturalists are hoping to increase the numbers of trumpeter swans raised in the wild by secretly placing trumpeter eggs (which can cost $200 each) in the nests of mute swans. Unfortunately, mute swan cygnets (young swans up to a year old) are brownish-gray, while trumpeter babies are white. When the eggs hatch, the naturalists retrieve the trumpeter cygnets long enough to color their down feathers so that the mute parents won't reject them. It hasn't been very successful, and it does nothing to help teach the trumpeter babies to migrate—mute swans don't migrate.

There's no telling yet whether these unusual methods will work, but many people are trying to help endangered species recover in whatever way they can.

Chapter 2

Species and Catastrophe

EXTINCTION OF SPECIES is nothing new. It's been part of the repeating pattern on Earth since life began.

A *species* is a group of plants or animals that are capable of mating and producing new young. All humans are one species because we can all mate with each other.

No one knows for sure just how many different species there are on Earth. There might be 10 million. There might be 20 million, 30 million, or more. Most of them are plants. However, only about 1.7 million plants and animals have actually been given names and classified, or sorted into categories of related organisms.

A botanist from the Smithsonian Institution thoroughly studied a piece of Malaysian rain forest only 0.2 square mile (0.5 square kilometer) in area. He found 835 species of trees, more than are found in all of the United States and Canada.

FACT

Where did all these species come from? Scientists believe that they gradually evolved over time. *Evolution* is the process by which new species develop from older ones. Genes are the chemical patterns in living cells that control the way an organism develops from fertilized egg to adult. Sometimes when cells reproduce, an accident happens and a gene fails to match itself perfectly. This event is called a mutation.

Many mutations are harmful and the affected plant or animal fails to reproduce. But occasionally a mutation occurs that makes the adult function better than others of its species.

For example, perhaps one of the early finchlike birds of

Because the Everglades snail kite eats only a specific type of green snail, it is not adaptable to habitat changes. The disappearance of the snail would mean extinction for the kite.

ancient Hawaii was hatched with a slightly narrower bill than the other birds had. This mutation might have allowed the bird to eat better because it could get its bill into narrower places. If it ate better, it might have been able to reproduce more offspring than the other birds did. Some offspring might have inherited the narrow bill from their parents, so they too might have had an advantage over other birds.

Charles Darwin, who helped develop the idea of evolution of species, called this process *natural selection*. Chance genetic mutations combine with factors in the environment to bring about the evolution and extinction of species.

One of two things may have happened next to the Hawaiian birds. The new form may have been strong enough to overwhelm the original species, which gradually disappeared from the population because they did not leave many offspring behind. Or, instead of replacing the old form of beak, the new variety might have been able to move on to a different habitat, and the original species did not disappear.

In the first case, the original species changed over time to one with a narrow beak. In the second case, a new species formed, distinct from the first, but the original continued to exist as well.

A plant or animal that is suited to its environment is said to be well adapted. A species can be well adapted by being a specialist—by being very good at making its living in one particular way—or by being a generalist, a jack-of-all-trades. Which strategy will work best depends on the environment or habitat it lives in.

Specialized Eaters

Some animals are endangered or threatened because they eat only a certain kind of food, which is also in danger. These specialized eaters are particularly vulnerable when humans interfere with the environment the species evolved in. The Everglades snail kite lives on a certain freshwater snail. The giant panda eats only bamboo. The ivory-billed woodpecker (which may well be extinct) eats only magnolia fruit and the grubs of the longhorn beetle.

Check out the food habits of the birds in your yard or a nearby park by setting up feeding stations. Wooden trays with sides or pie tins hung from the lower branches of a tree will do. If there are no trees, attach a feeder to a pole driven into the ground. Either way, it will not be squirrel proof—but squirrels need to eat, too.

Put different food in each tray, such as sunflower or thistle seeds, cracker crumbs, cracked corn, and mixed bird seed. Keep track of which tray contains which food. Spend as much time as you can observing from a distance. Record the number of birds and the different kinds that come to each station. Are there some birds that eat from each tray? Which trays do the squirrels prefer?

Sometimes the evolution of a particular characteristic seemed like an advantage at first, but then evolution went too far and the characteristic became a disadvantage. That happened with the great Irish elk. It had the largest antlers known, sometimes as wide as 13 feet (4 meters) across. Large antlers were an advantage at first. Perhaps larger-antlered elk were more successful at winning mates. But finally the large-antlered elk became too big to move through the thick forest. The species became extinct about 2 million years ago.

The *Orinoco crocodile* can be 20 feet (6 meters) — the longest crocodile in the world. It has become endangered because people treasure its hide.

Venezuela

Colombia

| Historic Range | Present Range |

In the past, extinctions were part of the evolutionary process. We know about many species that no longer exist by the fossil evidence left behind. However, such natural extinctions happened slowly, perhaps not more than once every thousand years. New species evolved to take their places.

Sometimes extinctions occur more quickly, even devastatingly, for many species at once. These mass extinctions were usually caused by a dramatic change in the environment.

The Dinosaurs

Paleontologists—scientists who study the fossil record of life on Earth—have learned that a major extinction took place about 248 million years ago. More than three-fourths of all species died out. But the event turned into an advantage for certain reptiles that survived the catastrophe. That extinction marked the beginning of the Age of Dinosaurs. Reptiles evolved in virtually every size and shape to take advantage of just about every kind of ecosystem on the planet—seas, deserts, swamps, lakes, and even air.

The dinosaurs lived long and successfully—and left enough remains behind to keep us perpetually fascinated by them. Then, about 65 million years ago, catastrophe struck again, wiping out dinosaurs within a short time.

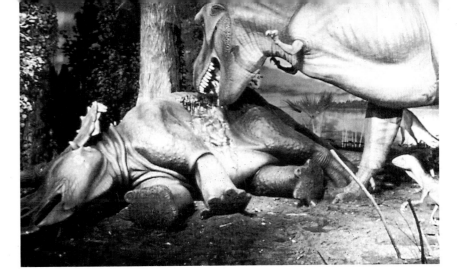

Just what happened was long a mystery to scientists, and theories of all kinds abounded. In recent years, however, scientists all over the world have found a very thin layer of metallic dust deep in the Earth. The dust is made up of the minerals found in meteorites—the rocks that occasionally fall to Earth from space.

That layer of dust has caused scientists to develop the current theory that a huge meteorite, or perhaps the rocky core of a comet, struck the Earth. The impact blasted the meteorite into dust, which blew high into the atmosphere around the planet. The dust completely blocked out the sun.

For many weeks the sky must have been darker than a moonless night. The warmth of the sun failed to penetrate the dust, and temperatures dropped. Huge wildfires roared across the planet, burning away the land's plant life. More than half of the species of land plants became extinct.

And the dinosaurs? There was nowhere for the beasts to hide. Within an incredibly short period, the results of more than 175 million years of evolution were gone. Just about the only survivors were some small mammals that had been able to burrow into the ground, a few dinosaur relatives that were beginning to venture into the skies, and some smaller reptiles that inhabited the oceans, such as sea turtles.

Amphibians in Danger

Amphibians (frogs, toads, and salamanders) were already well established on Earth by the time the dinosaurs became dominant, and they survived the great catastrophe that killed the giant reptiles. But they may not survive human beings. In fact, many amphibians have disappeared all over the planet, especially in areas where wetlands have been drained.

The problem is that amphibians require more than one habitat in order to complete their life cycle. They need water for egg laying and development as "teenagers," and adults need land to live on.

In early spring, go to a nearby pond or stream and collect frog eggs. Frog eggs are laid in jellylike masses that float on the water's surface. Collect about 20 eggs in a 1-gallon (3.8-liter) glass jar filled with water from the pond. Add a few strands of floating aquatic plants and some algae (green pond scum).

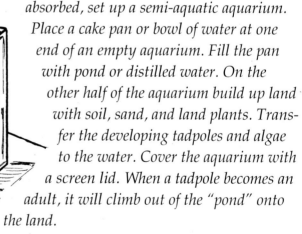

When the tadpoles begin to grow legs and their tails are being absorbed, set up a semi-aquatic aquarium. Place a cake pan or bowl of water at one end of an empty aquarium. Fill the pan with pond or distilled water. On the other half of the aquarium build up land with soil, sand, and land plants. Transfer the developing tadpoles and algae to the water. Cover the aquarium with a screen lid. When a tadpole becomes an adult, it will climb out of the "pond" onto the land.

Capture live insects and release them into the aquarium. If after a few days your frogs are still not eating, return them to their original environment.

The survivors of the mass extinction of reptiles and many other living things began to evolve into new species that once again took advantage of all the different habitats available on the planet. Among the new species of mammals that would eventually develop were large-brained primates that gradually began to walk on two feet and use their hands to manipulate their world. This new species was *Homo sapiens,* or human beings. Little did anyone know that these human beings would be the cause of Earth's next mass extinction.

The *Monte Verde toad* has not been seen in three years. It is probably extinct because its small rainforest habitat is being destroyed.

NICARAGUA

COSTA RICA

PANAMA

Historic Range

Present Range

The Human Catastrophe

Humans have a major attribute that allows them to do more things to the planet than any other species—a massive brain. Humans have used their brains to move into and take over every environment on the Earth. But in the process we have changed ecosystems until they were no longer habitable by other species. We have killed off other species for our own pleasure and food, often not even noticing when they were gone except to be a little annoyed.

We are the new catastrophe that is extinguishing Earth's living species. We are so busy reshaping the Earth to our own needs and wants that we've neglected to leave other species their share.

Millions of American buffalo (bison) were slaughtered by hunters in the 1800s with no regard for the survival of the species or the Native Americans who depended upon it.

Today, people are more aware of what they are doing, but it may be too late for many species. In 1991 biologist Paul R. Ehrlich, best known for his writing on the exploding human population, and Edward O. Wilson predicted that cutting down our rain forests could cause the disappearance of 25 percent of all Earth's species within the next 50 years.

FACT

A list of the vertebrates known to have become extinct in the United States and Canada in the last 500 years includes 39 mammals, 39 birds, 24 fish, 3 reptiles, and 1 amphibian. In addition, hundreds of invertebrates and probably thousands of plants have also disappeared.

Humans are the new comet striking the Earth. In the nineteenth century we used guns and axes. Today, we're more subtle but no less effective. We let our cities expand far out into the countryside. Our chemicals pollute the land, sea, lakes, and air. The environmental stresses we've created far outweigh the development of mutations that can handle them. Species are becoming extinct at an alarmingly fast rate.

The comet had no power to change its path before devastating the life on Earth, but we do.

Kemp's Ridley Sea Turtle

Sea turtles were among the animals that survived the catastrophe that ended the Age of Dinosaurs, but they may not survive the Age of Man. All but one of the six species of sea turtles are endangered, and Kemp's ridley is the most critically endangered of all.

Kemp's ridley sea turtle is about 2 feet (61 centimeters) long, smallest of the sea turtles. Its shell and skin are dark greenish-gray, and the bottom shell is colored a lighter version of the same color. Kemp's ridley lives in the Gulf of Mexico, especially along the shores of Texas and Mexico. It is very long lived, perhaps reaching 60 years—unless it runs into humans.

When a female turtle is ready to lay eggs, she lumbers slowly across a sandy beach, digs a hole with her flippers, deposits her eggs, covers them, and heads back into the sea. The golf ball-sized eggs hatch in the warm sand. When the tiny baby turtles emerge, they crawl to the sea and begin their aquatic life. Unfortunately, one of the things that draws the babies from far up on the beach into the water is the brightness of the sea compared to the land. In many places human night life is brighter than the sea, and the babies are drawn toward roads and buildings.

If they make it safely to the water, they will probably not return to the beach for at least fifteen years, when they come as mature adults. Each female lays about 100 eggs. However, it's estimated that only about 1 percent of all hatchlings live to return to the beach.

The female's awkwardness on the beach is quickly forgotten in the sea—the turtles' natural element. Like birds

Each year from 1978 to 1988, approximately 2,000 Kemp's ridley sea turtle eggs were shipped to Padre Island National Seashore, Texas, for incubation. The eggs hatched after 48 to 55 days (top left). The young hatchlings were released on the beach and entered the surf (top right) so the characteristics of the Padre Island beach would be imprinted (established) in their brains. Biologists hope adult turtles — imprinted as hatchlings — will return to the same beach habitat in 12 to 14 years to lay their eggs. After release, the hatchlings were recaptured and transferred to a laboratory to grow for 10 months (middle). The tagged turtles were released again 10 miles (16 kilometers) offshore, and biologists hoped that mature turtles would return to nest. But only one Kemp's ridley sea turtle (without a tag or tag scar) nested at Padre Island National Seashore in April 1991 (bottom left).

flying through the air, turtles fly through the water. They travel the oceans for crabs, fish, mollusks, and even jellyfish.

One of the great dangers sea turtles face occurs even as they swim. Sailing out of the ports along the Gulf of Mexico are numerous shrimp boats. They drop huge nets as they trawl along shallow water, hoping to scoop up vast quantities of shrimp. Sea turtles are often scooped up along with numerous unwanted fish. It's estimated that for every pound (0.4 kilogram) of shrimp caught, about 10 pounds (4.5 kilograms) of unwanted living creatures are also caught.

Not that sea turtles are unwanted. They have long been caught for their tasty meat and beautiful shells, which can be cut and polished into ornaments. Japan has made ornaments from about 2 million sea turtles in just the last 20 years.

Since 1987, U.S. fishing boats have been required to use turtle excluder devices (TEDs) on their nets during the part of the year when nesting turtles are in the shallow water. These devices allow the turtles to avoid the nets, along with many valuable shrimp, according to the fishermen. A 1990 study showed that TEDs should be used all year round. The shrimpers are protesting, and the controversy continues.

A film made in 1947 on a Mexican beach showed about 40,000 adult females coming ashore to lay eggs. But all along the Gulf of Mexico, the beaches have been taken over by humans. The only known major nesting site left is at Rancho Nuevo, in the state of Tamaulipas, Mexico, where fewer than 350 adults were seen in 1990. Since 1978, eggs were taken from Mexico and incubated in sand on Padre Island off the coast of Texas. The resulting 12,000 young were released on Padre in the hope that some adults would live to return there to nest. Scientists wait to see.

Chapter 3

Lost Homes and Habitats

LET'S DO SOME CALCULATING.

Ten thousand years ago there were probably no more than 10 million human beings on the planet. That's fewer people than live in any of at least 12 metropolitan areas around the world today.

The surface of the Earth is about 196,800,000 square miles (509,700,000 square kilometers) in area. Therefore, when agriculture was invented, there was one human for every 20 square miles (52 square kilometers) of the Earth—both land and ocean. (Of course, humans don't generally live in the ocean, but we'll ignore that fact for the moment.)

Estimates of the number of species that may exist on Earth range from 10 million to 80 million. We'll use a figure of 40 million. Therefore, one human shared 20 square miles of the planet with only about 5 other species. There was plenty of room for everyone.

In 1992, there were about 5.4 billion people on Earth—one human for every 0.036 square mile (0.9 square kilometer), or 27.4 people per square mile (2.5 square kilometers). But there were still about 5 species in that square mile—or at least there used to be. People—and their homes, farms, buildings, deserts, parks, football stadiums, parking lots, and highways—no longer leave much room for other species.

If you remember that less than one-third of Earth's surface—only about 57,900,000 square miles (149,000 square kilometers)—is land, that really means that there are now 93 people per square mile.

Even more devastating than the sheer numbers of people on the Earth, however, are what those people do. When it comes to a fight between humans and other species, humans always win.

Ecosystems and Habitat

Every plant and animal species evolved to live in a specific setting. All aspects of that setting, including other living things, interact to make just the right home, or *habitat.*

Some of the attributes of a habitat that may be important include the water supply, the mineral content of that water, periodic flooding, the amount of sunlight, the regularly recurring winds or rains, the content of the soil, the height of surrounding trees, insects that pollinate flowers, the availability of nesting materials, safety for raising young, and the amount of territory available for roaming in search of food.

Such a habitat may be found within a specific ecosystem—a northern river floodplain, perhaps, or a pine forest, or a warm tropical sea.

Every aspect of a habitat—as well as every habitat within a total ecosystem—can be damaged by human beings.

Pollutants from factories can damage water. Building a housing development on a floodplain can limit the amount of water that reaches a wetland area. Building a skyscraper near a mountain can block sunlight and winds. Spraying pesticides can prevent certain flowers from being pollinated. Building a highway can cut an animal's territory in half.

Is it any wonder that so many species and populations of plants and animals are in danger?

The *harpy eagle* nests in the tops of the tallest rainforest trees. The destruction of rainforests and illegal hunting threaten its survival.

Historic Range

Present Range

Sowing Seeds to Repair Habitat

An Earth Experience

Tall grasses and prairie flowers provide food, shelter, and nesting grounds for a lot of wildlife. These plants have lost ground to cultivated crops and suburban lawns. However, numerous places can be seeded if caring people will just take the time and energy.

First locate several sites in your neighborhood, town, and community where you would be allowed to sow some seed. A vacant lot, school grounds, nearby wetlands, a roadside, or an artificial pond near a condominium or office building would be good places to start. Get permission from the owners before you secure the seeds.

With assistance from a teacher or parent, you can order free seeds from many state departments of conservation when they know your plan. A number of preserves, nature centers, and arboretums will permit seed collection in the fall under supervision. They will provide instructions on how to germinate and plant the seeds.

Tall grasses such as big bluestem, Indian grass, and switch grass provide cover and food for the prairie chicken, pheasant, meadowlark, and prairie dog. Muskrats eat cattails around a wetland and use them to build their homes. Wood ducks nest in trees along the bank of a stream. Many flowering plants provide a source of food for insects. All links in the food chain can be helped with this project.

Study the list of endangered species, their habitats, and food choices. Do your part in replacing the plants they need. There are many corners of the world and unplanted habitats where you can sow seeds and help wildlife survive on this crowded planet.

Decisions from On High

Frequently, construction projects have destroyed a species of plant or animal that had a limited range. It's probably happened more often than we know because the species was gone before we even knew it was endangered. In recent times, however, especially in industrialized nations, conservation-minded people have become better informed. They are more aware when a species is threatened and try to prevent its extinction.

Because the United States, like many other countries, has laws protecting endangered species (see Chapter 5), government officials sometimes have to make decisions concerning a habitat that will determine the final fate of a species or subspecies. At least 30 species of fish have become extinct in the United States, primarily because construction destroyed the single habitat where each species was able to survive. A similar case of a mammal being in danger of extinction because of a construction project is that of a red squirrel.

Mount Graham Red Squirrel. Usually scientists are on the side of the environmentalists, but they clashed over the building of an observatory on Mount Graham in Arizona. The 10,700-foot (3,200-meter) mountain, about 100 miles (160 kilometers) north of Tucson, was the perfect location, said scientists at the University of Arizona, for a group of seven telescopes to be used in studying the secrets of the universe.

But Mount Graham is the habitat of a subspecies of red squirrel that has lived in the spruce forest there for thousands of years. In June 1987, the U.S. Fish and Wildlife Service (USFWS) declared the red squirrel endangered. Its numbers were down to about 100.

Based on a report from the USFWS saying that the telescopes and the squirrels could coexist on the mountaintop, the U.S. Congress granted the observatory project an exemption from normal rules that restricted development in the habitat of an endangered species.

Construction was ready to start when activists from the Earth First! organization chained themselves to some of the heavy equipment preparing a road up the mountain. At about the same time, two USFWS employees testified in a court hearing that they had been ordered by their superiors to write that report for Congress, knowing that it was not true. Even so, the federal appeals court ruled in 1991 that construction could go ahead—astronomy research was more important than the squirrel subspecies.

The little Mount Graham red squirrel has lived on the top of one mountain in Arizona for thousands of years. Now, its days may be numbered.

The Dusky Seaside Sparrow. Usually, many different factors combine to drive a species to extinction, with a final blow given by officials "on high."

The last known dusky seaside sparrow died at Disney World on June 16, 1987. This species, always small in number, had long found suitable habitat in the marshes near Merritt Island at Cape Canaveral, Florida.

Development of the area started in the 1950s when America's space program was getting started. Poisonous chemicals were sprayed to kill mosquitoes. Roads were built across the marshes. And the marshes themselves were drained, destroying the specific grasses that the dusky seaside sparrow needed to live.

In 1971, an effort was made to save the endangered bird

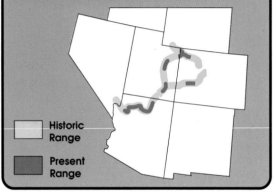

Numerous large water projects in the Colorado River Basin have destroyed most of the deep, fast-running water habitat of the *humpback chub.*

Historic Range

Present Range

by establishing St. John's National Wildlife Refuge, but still the water drained out of the marshes. Then, in 1973, the final blow fell. Ornithologists decided that the dusky seaside sparrow was a subspecies of sparrow, and not a separate species. Government funds to save endangered species were limited at that time to species only, so no effort was going to be made to save the bird.

A biologist with the Florida Audubon Society tried to rescue the few remaining birds from the marshes near Cape Kennedy. But all he could find were males. The last female was seen about 1975. The biologist tried to crossbreed the males with females of Scott's seaside sparrow subspecies. But the males were too old, and the eggs were infertile. Visitors to the Disney World zoo in June 1987 saw the last known dusky seaside sparrow.

An Earth Experience

Limited Space

Forcing wild things to live in too small a space reduces their numbers until they are threatened or disappear entirely. The following activity will demonstrate this idea.

Locate two pieces of plywood: one measuring 1 foot (30 centimeters) square and a second measuring 4 feet (1.2 meters) square. Find a secluded spot in your backyard or an open field where you can mark off two 4-foot (1.2-meter) -square areas. Count the number and kinds of each organism you find in each area. Look for ants, spiders, worms, grubs, larvae, beetles, sowbugs, and other creeping, crawling things.

Now place one board in each area. Place a rock on top of the boards so they will not be moved by an animal or the wind. Leave them in place for two weeks.

Now remove the boards, which represented habitat size. Once again count the animals you find. Compare the counts you get for each area. Does this tell you that the numbers and kinds of organisms go down when space is reduced?

One Fatal Step at a Time

More deadly to more species have been the millions of individual decisions that seemed right when they were made but turned out to be deadly for wildlife.

• A factory developer decides to run wastewater directly out of the plant into a river instead of installing a purification system. The pollution in the wastewater accumulates until nothing can live in the river.

• Households all over the country buy a new brand of cleanser that contains more chlorine for "whiteness." But the chlorine ends up in rivers and ponds, where it's poisonous.

• When farm prices go down, many farmers cut down the hedgerows along the edges of their farms in order to increase their cropland. When hedgerows are cut, thousands of little animals and plants have no place to go.

The killing of fish by pollution in waterways has become a common occurrence. An accidental chemical spill can kill portions of a river in a few hours. Repairing the damage, if possible, takes years.

• A suburban developer, hoping to get three or four more house lots out of his property, fills in a wetland area. With the wetland gone, migrating birds have fewer places to stop on their way north. They arrive exhausted and don't produce young.

• Pleasure boaters rip open bubble packaging on a piece of new equipment and throw the plastic overboard. Approximately 24,000 tons (21,700 metric tons) of plastic get into the sea each year. The bubbles look like jellyfish, which attract sea turtles. The turtles eat the plastic and die.

• A home gardener decides that his fruit trees aren't producing enough fruit, so he sprays them with pesticide. That decision was frequently made back in the middle of the twentieth century, and birds of prey, such as the peregrine falcon, have been suffering ever since.

Little by little, humans take over the habitats of plants and animals. Bit by bit, land inhabited by other species is made useless, and even poisoned, by human activity.

Most naturalists know that working hard to save a species is probably not as important as saving its habitat. However, habitat is not necessarily one place. Migrating birds, for example, need winter quarters with places to sleep and places to feed. Their summer quarters must provide the same things, as well as a quiet spot where they can lay their eggs and raise their young until they are big enough to fly. And, in between, they need still other habitats— good places to stop to rest and feed along the way.

All along the main migration routes (called flyways) followed by ducks, geese, and swans from Mexico to Canada, wetland areas have been drained for farmland and filled in for housing. The populations of waterfowl have shrunk drastically because of loss of habitat. Although few of the birds are on endangered lists yet, the sudden drop in their numbers was so alarming that, in 1986, the United States and Canada formed the North American Waterfowl Management Plan to develop new habitats along the birds' routes. Mexico joined later.

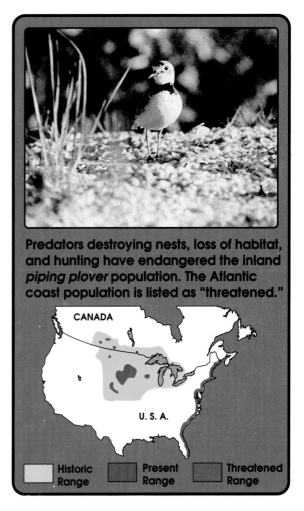

Predators destroying nests, loss of habitat, and hunting have endangered the inland *piping plover* population. The Atlantic coast population is listed as "threatened."

CANADA

U. S. A.

| Historic Range | Present Range | Threatened Range |

In 1983, a Wyoming rancher finished the long task of fencing his entire 20,000 acres (8,000 hectares). But the fence crossed the migration path that took the pronghorn antelopes, the fastest mammals in North America, to their traditional winter feeding ground, called Red Rim. Halted by the fence, the beautiful animals piled up against it, bewildered. As many as 1,000 pronghorns starved to death against the fence. The problem ended only when the state bought the ranch and destroyed the fence.

FACT

Ash Meadows. A huge area of wetland surrounded by desert along the California-Nevada border is called Ash Meadows. Almost 30 different species of plants and animals that exist nowhere else have been found there. In the 1950s, some species of fish that had been introduced in the area began to overwhelm the endemic species, driving them to extinction. In the 1960s, a huge farming operation threatened several more species because it removed too much water from the ground beneath the meadows. In the early 1980s, housing development made matters worse. Finally, in 1984, an organization called The Nature Conservancy bought almost 13,000 acres (5,200 hectares) of Ash Meadows, which are now part of the Ash Meadows National Wildlife Refuge.

The separate species living in Ash Meadows could not have been protected individually. They were endangered by adverse changes to their entire ecosystem, and it was only by protecting the whole ecosystem that they could be protected.

Buying Land to Preserve It. The Nature Conservancy has purchased land in many places in North and South America to protect a species and its habitat. In 1984, for example, the organization bought 13,000 acres (5,200 hectares) in Coachella Valley, California, to protect the only known habitat of the fringe-toed lizard. Later they found that they had also bought the only known habitat of a round-tailed ground squirrel.

In 1990, the Conservancy persuaded a farmer in Iowa to sell 44 acres (18 hectares) of his farm where a rare Pleistocene snail had a colony. Long thought to exist only as fossils, the snail was found still to be living on rocks above icy underground caverns located on the Iowa farm.

As more and more people move to southern Florida, the habitat on the Florida panther becomes smaller and smaller. Biologists do not expect the panther to survive.

Although little bits of habitat are being saved, sometimes that may not be enough. There may be factors affecting the habitat that we don't yet fully understand or that we cannot control.

Florida Panther. There are only about 30 Florida panthers left. This cougar (or mountain lion, or puma) subspecies once lived in large numbers throughout the southeastern states, but its habitat is now limited to a small area in the swamps of southern Florida. They were legally hunted until 1958. In 1967, the Florida panther was included on the first U.S. endangered list. It became a state felony to kill one in 1979. In 1982, it became the only endangered animal to be named a state animal.

Even though legal measures were taken to protect the panthers, new development continued. As millions of additional people moved into Florida, they needed housing, industry, water, agriculture, and recreation. This development has driven the few remaining Florida panthers into a smaller and smaller territory. And, because so much water is taken from under southern Florida to send to the growing cities, panther habitat is changing.

In the limited space remaining to the panthers, they have very few mates to choose from. One specialist says that 75 percent of the genetic diversity is gone. Because of such inbreeding, the male cats' sperm count is quite low, so the chances of a female getting pregnant are also low. Although protected, the Florida panther will probably not survive.

Butterflies and Beach Life

The Los Angeles area attracts many people, but it historically has attracted lots of butterflies, too. The Palos Verdes blue butterfly, found only in a few locations near Los Angeles, was listed as endangered in 1980. By 1982, only one of those sites was left, in the city of Rancho Palos Verdes. Unfortunately, the city built a baseball diamond on the site, and the blue butterflies were never seen again.

To prevent this from happening to another butterfly, the city of Los Angeles agreed in 1990 to preserve the last remaining piece of a major natural sand-dune system along the ocean. By doing this, they are preserving the habitat of the endangered El Segundo blue butterfly. Considering the

In Florida, recreational boats have caused widespread habitat and wildlife destruction (left). And the demand for water for urban growth and agriculture has left southern Florida with little good habitat for its wildlife (right).

amount of building that has gone on in the Los Angeles area, it's a miracle that the dunes still exist, but the 300-acre (120-hectare) area is located near Los Angeles International Airport, where, fortunately, people did not want to build.

A study lasting several years showed that the dunes were the only habitat of at least nine insect species and one flower species. The airport's noises and fumes do not seem to bother the vulnerable butterfly, though their effects over the long term are hard to predict. The sand-dune preserve will be replanted with some of the species that had disappeared over the years. These plants are expected to keep attracting the El Segundo blue butterfly.

The Monarch Butterfly. The monarch butterfly, also called the milkweed butterfly, is unique among insects—it migrates long distances—but not in the sense that the same butterflies travel south in the fall and back north again in the spring. Instead, two or three generations hatch and go through their metamorphosis each year in the United States and southern Canada. Only the last generation goes south. Those on the western side of the Rocky Mountains go to southern California. Those on the eastern side go to Mexico. When spring arrives, the insects quickly head north again to reach the places where milkweed grows. It is the only

Red howler monkeys live in small groups in South American rain forests. Each morning they howl to stake out their territory. Deforestation will silence them forever.

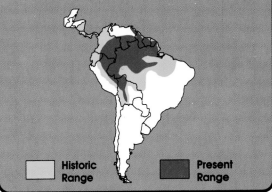

Historic Range
Present Range

plant on which monarch females lay their eggs. Few adults complete the return trip. Females lay eggs along the way and the offspring continue the journey.

The sight of many millions of black and orange butterflies in the sky at once is incredible. But that experience may soon become a thing of the past. Many wintering sites, particularly in California, have been destroyed by pesticides and other chemicals. Fewer than 45 wintering sites are known to exist, and they are right in the path of development. Most Mexican wintering sites are in nature preserves near Mexico City.

Combined efforts are being made to save the monarchs. At the local level, some plans are directed toward rescuing specific wintering locations. The town of Pacific Grove, which calls itself "Butterfly Town, U.S.A.," has had a law since 1939 against "molesting a butterfly in any way." Drivers must watch out for them when the butterflies are mating in October, often in the middle of the street. When a small pine and eucalyptus grove where millions of butterflies gather was about to be sold for development, the town passed a special tax to purchase the site.

At the state level, the California Department of Fish and Game manages the wintering sites.

Nationally, an effort is being made to designate the monarch butterfly the national insect of the United States. Being named the national insect doesn't automatically guarantee that the monarch will be saved, but certainly people will be slower to destroy its summer or winter habitats.

A Global Problem

The habitats discussed here have been fairly specific ones for specific plants and animals. There is another, bigger danger facing us, however—one that could harm human habitats, too. That danger is *global warming*.

The warmth that allows life to exist on our planet arises from a phenomenon called the greenhouse effect. Certain gases in air act like the glass in a greenhouse to hold heat in the atmosphere. The sun's radiation enters the atmosphere and strikes the surface of the planet. The rays are reflected back as shorter rays, called infrared, or heat rays. Those shorter rays can be absorbed by air molecules made up of three or more atoms. Carbon dioxide (CO_2) is a three-atom molecule, as is methane gas.

Such gases occur naturally in the air and have kept our planet relatively warm through many centuries. However, since humans started burning coal as an energy source for manufacturing, the amount of carbon dioxide has been building up in the atmosphere. Many scientists believe that

Beachfront development is a worldwide problem. The construction of this resort at Cancún, Mexico, may have destroyed irreplaceable nesting and breeding habitat for wildlife. Such land could be endangered by global warming.

this increase in CO_2 and other greenhouse gases is causing a global increase in the warmth of the planet that will become worse during the next decades.

The 1980s was the warmest decade and the winter of 1991-92 was the warmest on record, so those scientists may be right. Some scientists disagree, however. They say that such warm periods are just normal variations. Only time will tell who is right. But if the scientists who warn of global warming are right in their prediction, many more species are going to become endangered and extinct.

According to the World Resources Institute, 80 species already in danger of extinction can live only in a strip along coastal beaches from the water line to an elevation of about 10 feet (3 meters). This strip has already been severely dam-aged by beach development. Construction breaks the beach area into fragments, limiting the range of a species.

Global warming will make matters even worse because the sea will get warmer. Of course, warm water takes up more room than cold. That will make the level of the sea rise. That precious 10-foot strip will quickly be inundated by the sea. Where freshwater rivers meet the sea, the rising salt water will flow into freshwater rivers, destroying habitat.

In the United States alone, some of the already endangered species that live in or depend on those precious 10 feet above sea level include the little key deer of the Florida keys, the manatee, most sea turtles, a bird called the California clapper rail, the saltmarsh harvest mouse, and many wetland and sand-dune plants.

The central parts of the continents, such as North America's Great Plains, may also be in serious danger from global warming. They would likely suffer permanent drought. The temperature rise could force species to try to adapt to areas farther north, but not many of them would be able to adapt. Both crops and wild species could be seriously affected.

Endangered Spaces

The World Wildlife Fund of Canada is leading a 10-year program to protect the remaining natural ecosystems in Canada. The Endangered Spaces campaign was started in 1989 to develop a national park or other reserve in each of the recognized 350 natural regions of the country by the year 2000.

The organization, supported by over 150 other environmental groups around the country, has developed a Canadian Wilderness Charter (see the box on the next page). They collected the signatures of more than a million people who agreed with the prin-

Tourists visiting the Florida Keys threaten the remaining 250 to 300 *key deer*. Each year, the majority of deer killed (80 percent) are hit by vehicles on roads.

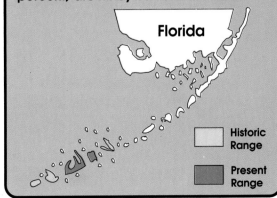

Florida

☐ Historic Range

■ Present Range

ciples and presented them to the government in the hope that at least 12 percent of Canada's land and water will be set aside.

Humans are the only animals that have the mental power to observe nature and appreciate its complexities. That ability sets us apart from other animals. And yet the mere fact that we can feel separate from nature—observing from "on high" rather than participating in it—is one of the main reasons we have done such damage to other living things and their habitats. Fortunately, we also have the ability to do something about it.

Thoughts from the
CANADIAN WILDERNESS CHARTER

- Humankind is just one of millions of species sharing planet Earth.
- The future of the Earth is severely threatened by the activities of this single species.
- Our planet has already lost much of its former wilderness character, thereby endangering many species and ecosystems.
- Canada's remaining wild places, be they land or water, merit protection for their inherent value.
- The protection of wilderness also meets an intrinsic human need for spiritual rekindling and artistic inspiration.
- Canada's once vast wilderness has deeply shaped the national identity and continues to profoundly influence how we view ourselves as Canadians.
- Canada's aboriginal peoples hold deep and direct ties to wilderness areas throughout Canada and seek to maintain options for traditional wilderness use.
- Protected areas can serve a variety of purposes including:
  —preserving a genetic reservoir of wild plants and animals for future use and appreciation by citizens of Canada and the world.
  —producing economic benefits from environmentally sensitive tourism.

The Peregrine Falcon

Just as World War II began, a Swiss chemist discovered that a chemical called DDT could kill insects on contact. After the war, it began to be used worldwide against disease-carrying pests, and the incidence of malaria, typhus, and yellow fever plummeted, as did crop infestations.

Something else began to happen, too, however. The poison began to accumulate in the bodies of certain animals. Birds of prey particularly were found to be producing eggs with shells so thin that they broke before they could be hatched. The reproduction rate of birds of prey—which are at the top of the food chain and thus accumulated more poison than other birds—dropped. The plight of two species became especially well known—bald eagles and peregrine falcons. These birds were seriously endangered before Rachel Carson, in her book *Silent Spring*, alerted the public. Eventually the use of DDT was banned in the United States, but it is still used elsewhere in the world.

The bald eagle is making a good recovery. It has been given top priority because it's the national bird of the United States. Also, there is a fairly large population of bald eagles in Alaska, where much less DDT was used.

Peregrine falcons aren't so lucky.

Peregrines are among the most fascinating birds of prey. Also known as duck hawks, their bodies average about 15 inches (38 centimeters) long and are gray-blue on the back and whitish on the breast.

The peregrine falcon population declined because the pesticide DDT built up in the bodies of the animals it ate, affecting reproduction.

They prey on other birds in flight and are especially drawn to shorebirds, which is one of the reasons their traditional migration paths follow Lake Michigan, the Mississippi, and both coasts.

Bill Cochran, sometimes called the "Birdman of Illinois," has spent years radio-tagging birds and following the radio signals to discover flight and migratory patterns. He has found that peregrine falcons generally spend about 17 hours of each 24 perching, 6 hours migrating, and 1 hour hunting. They migrate as much as 120 miles (193 kilometers) a day. When hunting they dive at speeds up to 200 miles (322 kilometers) per hour.

The program to breed peregrines in captivity and then release them in natural-like settings was started in the 1970s by Tom Cade of Cornell University when fewer than 100 pairs were left. Called hacking, the release process calls for putting chicks only a few weeks old in boxes mounted high on tall buildings. As the chicks grow, they look out over the world with the wide view they would have in natural cliffs. When the birds' flight feathers are matured, the cages are opened, and the birds are free to go. More than 3,000 birds have been released in North America, often in cities.

Many naturalists thought that peregrines could be the first endangered species to be removed from the list. But it was not to be. Ornithologists, in California especially, noticed that the birds were still not reproducing at a normal rate for the species and many dead birds were found to have high levels of toxic chemicals in their bodies.

Though DDT itself had been banned, chemicals made from it had not, and they were widely used in California's agriculture. Also, DDT and its breakdown product, called

Peregrine falcons can be bred successfully in captivity and released into the wild. This mother and chick are located high up on a city skyscrapter.

DDE, had been dumped in large amounts into California's harbors where they remained, getting into the food chain. Now the peregrine eggs may develop, but the chicks are born so contaminated that only about one-third of them live beyond the first year. And those that do live seem to have lost some of the survival instincts.

In 1989, a California laboratory tested some peregrine eggs and discovered that they contained five to ten times more dioxin than the amount known to kill an unhatched chicken. Dioxins are unintentional by-products of various other processes such as incineration. Scientists can usually identify the type of industry that produced dioxins by their chemical "fingerprints." But the dioxins that were killing the California's peregrine chicks were not specific. They were just poisons in the general environment, so nothing could be done to help.

The situation isn't any better inland. The egg failure rate among falcons that nest a long way inland is almost as high as for those along the coast.

No matter how humans work to keep the peregrine falcon alive, what we have done to its habitat already may have determined the final outcome for this magnificent bird.

Chapter 4

In the Name
of Business

WHEN EARLY HUMANS stopped being hunter-gatherers and settled in one place, they began to split up the tasks to be done for the community. Some people were responsible for feeding the others. That's when animals and plants became commercial products—things that bring in money.

And that hasn't changed since, although the prices have increased.

Loss to Commerce

There are many commercial uses for plants and animals. However, commercial use can wipe out a wild population.

When Europeans discovered the Gulf of St. Lawrence in the 1500s, they found hundreds of thousands of walruses living there. Then the Europeans discovered that the walruses' tusks were ivory, their hides made strong cable, and useful oil could be made from their blubber. Huge fleets of "factory" ships were sent to "mine" this new resource. And by the time the United States became a nation, there were no more walruses in the Gulf of St. Lawrence.

Treating Species as Trash

Sometimes a species just gets in the way of business. In the eastern Pacific Ocean, dolphins (porpoises) often swim with yellowfin tuna. These tunas are sold in cans and eaten worldwide. There's a big market for tuna, so fishermen have gone after them in a big way.

Tuna fishermen often locate schools of tuna in the Pacific by watching for dolphins. When they sight the playful mammals, they drop huge circular nets called purse seines behind their boats. A net sinks beneath a school of tuna and then

Dolphins and yellowfin tuna often swim together. Tuna fisherman have killed thousands of dolphins because their nets prevented the dolphins from rising to the surface to breathe.

gradually closes, pulling in hundreds of the fish.

Unfortunately, dolphins are caught, too. Because they are mammals, not fish, they must regularly rise to the surface to breathe air. But the nets hold them underwater and the dolphins drown. It's estimated that between 80,000 and 100,000 dolphins are killed every year by the nets of tuna fishermen. Dolphins are not yet on the endangered list, but at those numbers it probably will not be long.

In the United States, enough people complained about the senseless dolphin destruction that in 1990 the major tuna canners announced they would no longer buy tuna that had been caught with purse seine nets. The major North American brands of tuna now carry a "Dolphin Safe" label.

Japanese fishermen kill thousands of dolphins each year with little regard for the species' survival, regardless of the fact that they have no commercial value.

The American Tunaboat Association, however, insists that the action will do little to help the situation. They argue

that tuna fishermen from other countries are not affected by the ban and will simply sell their catches elsewhere, putting American fishermen out of work and raising the price of tuna in the United States. They also say that small tuna usually don't swim with dolphins. If small fish are the only ones caught, they can't grow up to reproduce, thus endangering the future of tuna fishing as a whole.

Animals as Pets and Souvenirs

There are thoughtless people in the world who think that somehow it's "cool" to own an endangered animal—or a part of the animal—and they are willing to pay for it. That means other thoughtless people are eager to capture endangered animals and sell them.

A major center for the sale of endangered species is Bangkok, Thailand, because Thai law protects only that nation's own animals. The animals are smuggled into Thailand across borders, and many of them die in the process.

Some animals are shipped with false papers indicating that they are destined for a nonexistent zoo. That makes the sale seem legitimate, and the animals are moved on to their destination and final sale. Also, because Thai law allows an individual to own two animals of an endangered species as pets, animal dealers often hire children to pretend that they own the animals and want to sell them.

Birds are sometimes transported by using legitimate papers for one kind of bird and then substituting a rarer species in the hope that customs officials can't tell the different kinds of birds apart.

The young of the last wild breeding pair of a Spix's macaw were kidnapped by an unscrupulous dealer and

South America's brown pale-fronted capuchin is threatened by poaching for the international pet trade.

eventually sold to a Swiss buyer. The buyer questioned where they came from, however, and in the nick of time the birds were rescued—just hours before they were to leave their native Brazil.

Because there are international penalties in most countries for dealing in endangered species, the criminals who sell them often put them in further danger by trying to smuggle them. Sometimes rare animals have been drugged and put into suitcases along with clothing, in the hope that they would survive an airplane flight. They rarely do.

A Japanese tourist traveling from Bangkok to Tokyo crammed 11 rare monkeys into a carry-on flight bag. Five of them were dead when he reached Japan and was caught.

Shirley McGreal, head of the International Primate Protective League, says that as many as 20 gibbons may die for each one that reaches the international market alive.

FACT

During the 1980s, the population of African elephants dropped by half because of the market for their ivory tusks. In January 1991, when 103 nations imposed a ban on the trade in ivory, the selling price of 2.2 pounds (1 kilogram) of ivory dropped from $200 to less than $5.

Although China's giant panda is severely threatened by loss of habitat, it is also stalked by hunters willing to kill for its beautiful and valuable fur (top). *Elephant ivory has been banned from international trade, but poachers still manage to slaughter large numbers because there is a market for ivory items such as this carved figurine* (bottom). *Some African countries are asking for reinstatement of elephant hunting.*

Pelts and Paws. Other animals are killed so that just part of them can be sold. Rhinoceros horns, for example, are sold for grinding up into medicines. Gorilla hands hold a fascination for some people who are willing to pay big prices for them.

The giant panda of China has long been in danger because its habitat was being destroyed. The thousand or so animals known to exist in the wild are now in more immediate danger of being killed for their beautiful fur pelts, for which people the world over are offering large amounts of money. China has instituted a death penalty for poaching pandas, but the law has little effect when a person can earn enough money to live on for a year by poaching one animal.

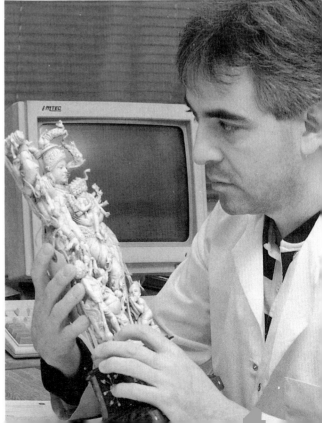

The U.S. Fish and Wildlife Service has opened a scientific laboratory for investigating crimes committed against endangered species—a world first. The facility is on the campus of Southern Oregon State College in Ashland, Oregon. This scientist at the laboritory is identifying a species through DNA fingerprinting—the pattern glows in ultraviolet light.

The International Effort. By 1992, 112 nations had signed the Convention on International Trade in Endangered Species of Wild Fauna and Flora, otherwise known as CITES. However, not all of them have passed the national laws necessary to back up the agreement. The point of CITES is to prevent trade in endangered species, but it is up to the individual countries to determine which species are listed. In the United States, each species listed as endangered goes on the international list.

Japan joined CITES in 1981, reserving the right to ignore the hawksbill sea turtles on the endangered list. Japan is known to have imported the shells of perhaps a quarter of a million hawksbill sea turtles since then. Hawksbills are treasured for their beautiful shells ("tortoiseshell"), which can bring about $500 per pound (0.4 kilogram). Japan finally gave in to world pressure and agreed to stop importing these endangered turtles by 1993.

During 1992, other nations began backing away from some of the CITES agreements. South Africa and several nearby nations, for example, want to "harvest" ivory from some of their elephants. They claim that by killing some elephants for commercial purposes, they will have the funds necessary to protect others from poachers.

If the CITES agreements continue to weaken, endangered species around the world that have commercial value may be in further jeopardy.

Commercial Use of Ecosystems

It's not just individual species that have been exploited to the brink of extinction. Whole ecosystems such as the rain forests of South America and Indonesia are being cut to such an extent that the numbers of species living within the forests are being devastated.

Just a few years ago, Canada had apparently endless forestland. But most of it has now been put under lease to logging companies to be cut in the next 20 or 25 years. Much of this area is inhabited by woodland caribou, wolves, bears, spotted owls, and other species that are already facing great difficulty.

Forestland is not an endless resource. Many Canadians are alarmed because most of their forests have been leased to logging companies.

In the past, only about a quarter of the cut forests were replanted, and less than half of the planted seedlings survived. By 1900, Canadian and industrial officials acknowledged that they must reforest if the industry was going to have long-term

14

survival. And yet, because no one truly believed that there would someday be a problem, they spent the next fifty years arguing about who was going to pay for the reforesting.

An organization that is concerned about saving the trees, Canada's Future Forests Alliance, notes, "This is the biggest crisis facing our future. In the next 15 years we're going to take down the whole ecosystem of the nation, and we don't even know the effect of this."

Even when forests are replanted, they are usually planted with just one species, and spaced so that tall, straight trees will grow. Undergrowth—in which numerous species live—is not allowed to accumulate in such "tree farms." And large amounts of fertilizers and insecticides are used to protect the growing trees. These chemicals poison the water and end up in the food chain of animals that enter the forests.

Business rights versus nature's rights is going to be a major topic of discussion during the coming years. Humans have always regarded Earth's resources as human resources, and now the Earth's resources are running out. We must protect what we have left.

Grizzly bears need large areas of roadless land where oil drilling, logging, and housing developments are not allowed. Although grizzlies are endangered in the lower 48 states because of deforestation and development, Alaska and Canada still have some time to protect grizzly bear habitat.

The Beluga, or White Whale

The cold waters around the coasts of Canada, Alaska, and Russia are the home of a very special sea-going mammal—the beluga. Sometimes called the white whale, the beluga is related to the narwhal. Both of these whales, unlike all other whales, are capable of moving their head separately from their body. The beluga's Latin name means "dolphin without a wing" because it has no dorsal fin.

Tan or gray baby belugas gradually turn white and adult belugas may be about 13 feet (4 meters) long and weigh up to 1 ton (0.9 metric ton). Social animals, they communicate by whistles. Like dolphins, they find their way around by a kind of sonar system, or echolocation. They make clicking noises that echo back, telling them the placement and size of objects in the water.

Belugas have served as the basic food of Inuit Eskimos for several thousand years. They provide high-energy meat, useful fats and oils, and leather. However, in the last 200 years, hunters from distant nations discovered the white whales and began to harvest them in large numbers. The

Canadian government banned commercial whaling in 1972, but it was almost too late for the populations that live in the estuary of the St. Lawrence River, in Ungava Bay in northern Quebec, and in Cumberland Sound, south of Greenland (the darker areas on the map below). These groups have only 400 or 500 animals each.

Of course, it hasn't been just hunting that has depleted the populations so badly. In the St. Lawrence particularly, the beluga habitat has been threatened by development on shore and contamination by chemicals. Their bodies have accumulated toxic substances that may have traveled long distances. For example, the whales eat eels that make their way from the Great Lakes out to the sea to spawn.

The St. Lawrence belugas have an additional problem in that they often swim past the Saguenay River to within 40 or 50 miles (64 to 80 kilometers) of the big city of Quebec.

Endangered beluga whale populations (represented by the green areas on the maps) live in the St. Lawrence estuary, in Ungava Bay in northern Quebec, and in Cumberland Sound, south of Greenland. Other beluga populations (represented by the aqua areas) are threatened.

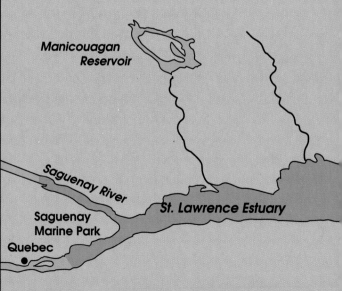

The establishment of Saguenay Marine Park is one step in protecting the St. Lawrence beluga. Dealing with industrial pollution in the St. Lawrence and Saguenay Rivers will ensure its survival.

Pleasure boating is a popular activity in the region. The motors of the high-speed boats give off noises that interfere with the whales' echolocation. In addition, people who "whale-watch" as a hobby often come upriver and disturb the fascinating animals.

The Canadian Department of Fisheries and Oceans, working with other departments, has established an "Interdepartmental Action Plan to Favour the Survival of the St. Lawrence Beluga Whale." They are studying the whale's migration patterns, genetic stock, and effect on other enterprises in an area. They also need to know just how water pollution affects the animals, as well as how the pollutants build up in the Inuits who depend on belugas for their food.

In 1990, the governments of Canada and the province of Quebec agreed to preserve the primary habitat of the St. Lawrence beluga by establishing a marine park where the St. Lawrence and Saguenay rivers meet.

Canada's Saguenay Marine Park was created in 1990 to protect the remaining St. Lawrence beluga whales. Pollution from heavy industry and development along the St. Lawrence River caused the whale population to decline.

Chapter 5

Endangered Species and the Law

EARLY EXPLORERS WERE STUNNED by the amount of wildlife they found in the New World. They were certain that they had found a living treasure chest that would last forever. But settlers had been in New England less than 75 years before the first laws were passed to preserve a species. In 1694, Massachusetts passed a law banning deer hunting for part of the year to ensure good hunting the rest of the year. The settlers didn't believe they would ever run out of game.

In the following years, other colonies, states, and nations prohibited the destruction of certain plants and animals that were special to their area. Eventually, this idea led to the establishment of the first national park—Yellowstone—in 1872, and the first national wildlife refuge—Pelican Island—in 1903. The idea was to preserve part of a country, especially an area endowed with rare living things. But construction, agriculture, highway building, wetland draining, and pollution continued all around the national parks.

Now we know that all living things are special, and that they can be destroyed unless attention is paid to them.

American Laws

Various wildlife conservation laws were passed regularly after about 1900, when President Theodore Roosevelt called Americans' attention to the plight of wildlife. But the real work of conservation did not get started until 1940, when the U.S. Fish and Wildlife Service (USFWS) was formed from two other agencies—the Bureau of Fisheries and the Bureau of Biological Survey. Working under the control of the Department of the Interior, it is the task of the USFWS to manage and protect the fish and wildlife resources of the United

States. In 1966 it became responsible for the protection of endangered species.

The main law under which endangered species are protected now is the Endangered Species Act (ESA) of 1973. It makes the basic assumption that plant and animal species are of "aesthetic, ecological, educational, historical, recreational, and scientific value to the Nation and its people."

The act requires the federal government to protect all plant and animal species that are endangered or threatened, *without regard to the economic impact of such protection.* It also requires the government to draw up plans for helping endangered species to recover, and calls for identifying and protecting "critical habitat" which would be important to protecting the species. The National Marine Fisheries Service is in charge of endangered ocean species.

The 1973 act makes it illegal for anyone to "take" a specimen of an endangered species. The word "take" covers attempting to take, collecting, pursuing, wounding, harassing, hunting, molesting, capturing, killing, or harming in any other way.

The act defines an *endangered* species as "any species which is in danger of extinction throughout all or a significant portion of its range." A *threatened* species is one that is "likely to become endangered within the foreseeable future throughout all or a significant portion of its range."

Up to 12 miles (19 kilometers) of fishing nets are lost in the ocean each day. The plastic or nylon nets don't deteriorate so they cause injury and even death to innocent animals, many of them endangered or threatened. This California sea lion, seriously wounded by a net, will probably die.

Another word often used is "extirpated," which means that a species is extinct in one country but exists in another. The black-footed ferret, for example, has been extirpated in Canada but exists in the United States.

In North America, a species might be in danger in the United States but not at all in Canada. The grizzly bear, for example, is almost gone in the United States except in Alaska. The main populations remaining in the lower 48 states exist in Yellowstone and in northern California.

The USFWS maintains a list of endangered and threatened species worldwide that currently includes about 1,135 plants and animals. About 620 of them are found in the United States. The Canadian list includes less than 200 species. The remainder live in other countries, but because they appear on the U.S. list, it is illegal for Americans to trade in these foreign species. The U.S. Endangered Species Act prohibits the importing or exporting of any endangered species.

The Endangered Species Act sets down a strict legal process by which a species gets onto the endangered list. Completion of the process takes the form of a law, so the process must be followed very closely.

We will learn more about the process by following the actual 1991 listing of the famous Snake River sockeye salmon.

The *giant otter* is 6.5 feet (2 meters) long, including the tail, and may weigh up to 88 pounds (40 kilograms). Illegal poaching for the otters' fur has threatened it.

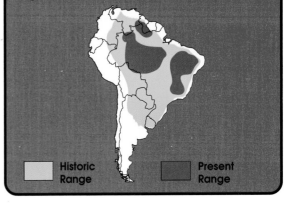

Historic Range

Present Range

The Sockeye Salmon

Sockeye salmon are large silvery fish, weighing about 60 pounds (27 kilograms). They spend most of their lives in the ocean but return to the rivers where they hatched to breed and start a new generation. They have to swim upstream (against the current), sometimes for long distances.

The sockeye salmon turns red when it is ready to breed, which is why the lake in Idaho where Snake River sockeyes breed is called Redfish Lake. To reach it, the sockeyes have to enter the Columbia River near Astoria, pass four dams, enter the Snake River, and then pass four more on the Snake. Finally, having traveled a distance of about 900 miles (1,450 kilometers)—as well as climbing more than 1 mile (1.6 kilometers) in altitude—the fish arrive at Redfish Lake in Idaho.

In Redfish, the females lay eggs in the shallow gravel. The eggs hatch in three or four months. Young fish, called smolts, stay in the lake for one to three years, until an internal clock tells them it's time to make their way to the sea.

Then the real trouble begins. Those eight water-power dams are waiting for the unwary fish, like traps. Many fish are caught in the turbines of the hydroelectric power plants. These propeller-like devices easily grind up fish.

Behind each dam is a reservoir of water, with quiet pools that attract the fish. There they become prey to wild animals. They become vulnerable to diseases, and, most important, their internal clocks go haywire. Instead of spending seven or eight days on the journey to the sea, they may be caught up for weeks. A natural mechanism in salmon that go to sea prepares their bodies for the switch from fresh water to salt water. When they stop along the way, the mechanism does its job anyway, and they die in the fresh water. Other fish lose the urge to migrate and the mechanism never kicks in.

The U.S. Army Corps of Engineers, which is in charge of America's waterways, actually collects the smolts in barges and trucks to transport them to the sea. For some unknown reason, not many of these fish are returning to the rivers.

One hundred years ago, the sockeye salmon industry harvested 4.5 million pounds (2 million kilograms) of fish each year. But in 1990 not a single red sockeye salmon was seen in Redfish Lake. Many people thought it was extinct.

Getting the Sockeye Salmon Listed

The Shoshone-Bannock Indians of Idaho, who have long depended on the sockeye salmon, petitioned the National Marine Fisheries Service to list the salmon as endangered in order to preserve the few remaining fish. The service started a biological investigation of the species, which included

Some dams are built with "fish ladders," which provide a rushing stream that allows the fish to bypass the huge structures.

69

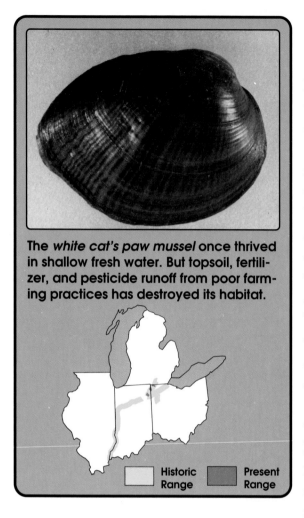

The *white cat's paw mussel* once thrived in shallow fresh water. But topsoil, fertilizer, and pesticide runoff from poor farming practices has destroyed its habitat.

Historic Range   Present Range

library research of all the references to the salmon since it was first commercially fished a hundred years before.

An important part of the research involved the salmon's *critical habitat.* Critical habitat is the area occupied by a species that contains the physical and biological features necessary to conserve the species. To determine this, biologists research which specific areas are of key importance in rebuilding the species. They evaluate the economic effect of designating an area as critical habitat, and then a final decision of the area is made.

By law, the people who decide what to list cannot ignore critical habitat, regardless of the economic impact, if doing so results in the extinction of the species. Among the factors in designating critical habitat is whether a specific place plays a unique role in the species' life history. For example, if an animal must migrate in order to breed, the migration route must be protected. Migration is a very important part of the salmon's life.

A "Salmon Summit" held in late 1990 was attended by all parties that play a role in the Columbia River Basin, which includes the Snake River. Each group agreed to review the effect their own structures and procedures have on the salmon. The Corps of Engineers, for example, said that water flow from dams could be increased to help speed migration.

After the full scientific review, papers were written giving the complete known history of the commercial value of the fish, the biology of its life, and the history and structures of the dams. They also analyzed the possibility that today's sockeye salmon is actually a hybrid with a different kind of salmon (the USFWS decided it wasn't). The papers were published as "proposed rules" in the *Federal Register* on April 5, 1991.

On November 14, 1991, the Snake River sockeye salmon was officially added to the list of endangered species.

After the official listing, a recovery plan is developed and implemented, directed at eventually removing the species from the endangered list. The critical habitat for the sockeye includes the entire Redfish Lake and the migration routes to and from the ocean. Everyone from Indian tribes to the people who control the dams will be involved in the process. The hope is that someday the sockeye salmon will be so abundant that Redfish Lake will live up to its name and once again teem with red fish.

Idaho's Native American attorney general, Larry Echohawk, helps children light candles to watch for sockeye salmon at the fourth and final Salmon Vigil at Redfish Lake Creek on August 17, 1991.

Problems with the Endangered Species Act

The theory of listing sounds wonderful. Unfortunately, the protection supposedly guaranteed the listed species often doesn't work. For example, recovery plans have no time schedule attached to them. Of the more than 600 U.S. species currently on the endangered list, almost half have never had recovery plans developed. A species without a plan to be followed is a species that probably will not survive, let alone recover. At least 18 species on the 1973 list are extinct, though some may have been gone before the list was made.

Numerous other species aren't even listed yet. Some authorities say that there are at least 4,000 endangered plants and animals that have not yet been listed. As many as 295 species have been identified as becoming extinct after they were put on the waiting list.

The USFWS notes that "endangered means there is still time." But if nothing productive is done with that time, both the time and the species will be lost.

The problem, of course, is that the Fish and Wildlife Service has neither the personnel nor the funding to get a species listed, prepare a recovery plan, or carry out the recovery plan. Sometimes the only way a species gets listed is to have its forthcoming extinction arise as an emergency, or because someone goes to court to get a species listed.

Unfortunately, the U.S. government is not very decisive about saving species, and it reflects the opinion of the American people. When first passed in 1973, the Endangered Species Act was the strongest environmental protection measure in the world. Then, in 1978 it was weakened by allowing a special committee to decide to ignore a species' plight if the cost to human activities was thought to be too great. The committee has been called the "God squad" because it has the power of life or death over endangered species.

In 1986 the act was weakened again, and in such a way that the United States appears to the world to be very two-faced. We protect our own species, but the government decided that we did not have to give the same protection to species outside our borders. If, for example, the U.S. financially supports a program to spray pesticides over a large area of a Latin American country, no consideration has to be given to the effect on local species. In effect, Americans are telling people in other countries that their wildlife doesn't count.

In the early 1990s, more and more people were complaining about the effect of the Endangered Species Act and other environmental laws on their lives. There was a move afoot in 1992 to change the act so that economic benefits would be more important than environmental ones in listing a species. This would completely destroy the usefulness of the act.

The *jabiru stork* is one of the longest birds (4.5 feet or 1.37 meters) in the world. Wetland drainage and illegal shooting have threatened these shorebirds.

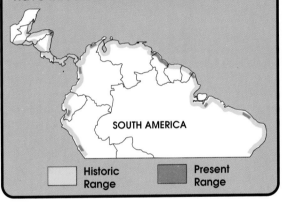

SOUTH AMERICA

Historic Range   Present Range

Endangered Plants

Animals, especially large ones, generally make noises, bleed, look grand, and otherwise get themselves noticed. Not so with plants.

Since species first started being protected, plants have stayed pretty much at the bottom of the list unless they are very famous or imposing.

Many people find it difficult to worry about a small plant hidden under a tall tree or behind a rock. Some plants exist in only a few small patches tucked away in suburban areas where an off-road vehicle or erosion from nearby development can readily destroy them. Others are found in a single patch at the mouth of a mountain cave.

The difficulty with getting people interested in plants is reflected in the way the federal government spends money for endangered species. Plants get only 8 percent of all USFWS funds spent on endangered species, although almost half of all listed endangered or threatened species (and about two-thirds of those waiting to be listed) are plants.

Many of Hawaii's birds appeared on the original endangered list, but the plants were ignored. Only 19 endangered plant species were listed in 15 years although almost 500 Hawaiian plant species were waiting to be listed. At the rate USFWS was reviewing them—species by species—it would have taken more than 100 years to study them all. By then, they'd be extinct.

The importance of quick listing is that when it is done, a plant cannot

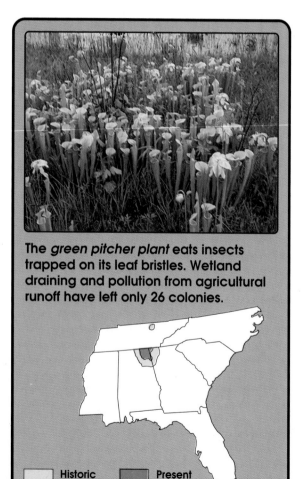

The *green pitcher plant* eats insects trapped on its leaf bristles. Wetland draining and pollution from agricultural runoff have left only 26 colonies.

Historic Range   Present Range

Endangered plants can be bred "in captivity" like animals. A group of botanists reintroduce Texas snowbells—grown at the San Antonio Botanical Garden—back into the wild.

be dug up, paved over, allowed to be eaten by animals, or anything else—even on private land. In 1990, as a result of a lawsuit, the 500 Hawaiian species were rearranged into a classification that left 186 species. The USFWS agreed to have 50 of them listed within a few months and the remaining 136 listed within two years.

In the 1988 version of the Endangered Species Act, the U.S. Senate instructed the USFSW to pay more attention to plants and lower animals. But that hasn't happened.

Saving Plants. How does the USFSW or a state agency go about rescuing an endangered plant? Basically, more easily and more cheaply than rescuing an animal. First, they may stop development where specific populations of the endangered species live. They search for other populations and try to protect them. They research the plant to find out just what its needs are, especially its habitat needs, to see if it will grow in other places. And they try to grow, or propagate, more plants so that they can be distributed over new areas.

In the long run, probably the only answer is to physically move endangered plants to a protected area. For some plants that will not work. They are just too big or too specific in their habitat needs—or even too old. The saguaro cactuses of

The last known Hawaiian gardenias grow in a plant sanctuary on Molokai, Hawaii. By 1994, 35 percent of all endangered plants will be Hawaiian species.

Hawaii

Historic Range

Present Range

the Southwest are very old and very fragile—and tempting to thoughtless people who think it's smart to use them for shooting practice. It would be sad if the only saguaros left had to be kept behind glass to preserve them.

There is the additional, and even bigger, problem that we don't really know enough about the habitats of certain plants to be sure that we're moving them to the right place. Certainly we can match up weather and soil and water and sunlight. But we don't know whether a plant needs certain insects to propagate, or perhaps a brief period of dryness for the plant to flower. Only by studying each endangered plant can we learn those things, and it may be too late.

The Center for Plant Conservation was created in 1984 to keep track of endangered plants and to oversee the development of gardens to grow endangered species. Originally located at Harvard University, it has been moved to St. Louis, Missouri.

Canada

Canada has not had a national program and laws concerning endangered species in the past because such matters were in the hands of the separate provincial governments. Canada has far fewer people per square mile than the United States, and vast areas of the country have never been inhab-

Canada's burrowing owl is a declining population due to the conversion of grasslands into croplands. Farmers also use insecticides to kill the owl and its insect prey.

ited by humans at all, except perhaps Eskimos and other Native Americans who lived in harmony with the land.

In 1976, the 40th annual Federal-Provincial Wildlife Conference passed a resolution calling for a committee of representatives from the provinces and federal governments and scientific organizations to determine the status of endangered and threatened species. Out of that resolution grew COSEWIC, the Committee on the Status of Endangered Wildlife in Canada. It is made up of representatives from each province, the federal government, and three large conservation organizations—the Canadian Wildlife Federation, Canadian Nature Federation, and World Wildlife Fund.

COSEWIC makes a decision about whether to list a species based on reports prepared by experts for the various committees, which are in charge of different categories of living things. In 1992 there were 195 species on the list, most from the heavily populated regions of southern Canada. Unfortunately, COSEWIC is a voluntary organization and few federal laws protect the species that get on the list.

The Canadian Endangered Species Recovery Fund was established in 1988 by COSEWIC and other organizations. These organizations are backing a program called RENEW, which stands for the Recovery of Nationally Endangered Wildlife. This is a movement to establish a national program with specific plans for the recovery of all endangered and threatened Canadian species. However, there is no funding.

In November 1991, the Wild Animal and Plant Protection Act was introduced in the House of Commons. Its main purpose, however, is to stop the importing of endangered species from other countries. It is unlikely to have much effect on Canada's own endangered species.

International Efforts

It has become clear in recent years that any kind of environmental protection can work only if all nations are involved. The Earth is one system, and what is done in one place affects the remainder of the planet.

The International Union for the Conservation of Nature and Natural Resources (IUCN)—usually called the World Conservation Union—is a semi-official body made up of

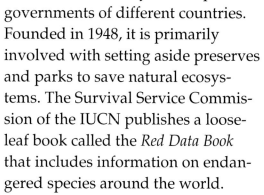

governments of different countries. Founded in 1948, it is primarily involved with setting aside preserves and parks to save natural ecosystems. The Survival Service Commission of the IUCN publishes a loose-leaf book called the *Red Data Book* that includes information on endangered species around the world.

Another important agreement among nations is CITES, the Convention on International Trade in Endangered Species of Wild Fauna and Flora. It will be discussed further in Chapter 6.

Many nations and organizations are working to preserve native wildlife through national parks and preserves. Lake Manyara National Park, Tanzania, protects many of the country's wildlife species such as these olive baboons.

The West Indian Manatee

Lumbering through the shallow waters of some of Florida's rivers are the few remaining sea mammals called manatees. Unlike any other creatures, these gentle, hulking, slow-moving mammals have graced the Earth's waters for at least 15 million years. Their very gentleness is their problem. They don't swim away in a flash, as a whale might. They don't snap and snarl, as an alligator does. They just kind of drift in midwater, without even the energy to escape from the blades of pleasure-boat propellers or the wisdom to look upward before surfacing to breathe. This gentle creature has no way to defend itself.

An adult manatee, also called a sea cow, may reach 13 feet (4 meters) long and weigh more than 1 ton (0.9 metric ton). Manatees are shaped a bit like bowling pins with flippers. They graze peacefully on water plants, never expecting danger. A female usually has only one baby every three years, which keeps manatee numbers from growing.

All of the West Indian manatee's relatives—two other

manatees and the dugong—are also endangered. Another relative, Steller's sea cow, which lived near Alaska, was extinct within 27 years after being discovered in 1741.

For a while in the nineteenth century, manatees were so plentiful that they were slaughtered and sold as "sea beef." There were plans more recently to import manatees to clear the Florida canals and rivers of water hyacinth, which has taken over many waterways.

But as early as 1893, Florida laws were beginning to protect these wonderful mammals. By 1907 there was a law giving prison sentences for harming a manatee. In 1978 the entire state was declared a manatee sancutary.

Attaching radio tags to manatees helps biologists study their behavior patterns. Human behavior patterns must change to save the manatee from pollution and boat propellers.

None of these measures worked, however. Almost 30,000 people move to Florida every month, most of them wanting to live near water. All those people add to the pollution entering the water, which kills the sea grasses on which the manatee feeds. Over one-third of all manatee deaths are due to collisions with recreational boats. Frequently they are mangled by propeller blades and die slowly.

Manatees are especially vulnerable in winter, when they tend to congregate around warm-water outlets on power plants and at natural springs. When that happens, a boat colliding with them may kill a dozen or more instead of just one. They are also endangered by swallowing plastic fishing line and other debris that gets into the water.

There are only about 1,400 manatees left in Florida's waters. There are probably 600 times that many power boats in Florida. It is projected that by the year 2000 there will be 1,600,000 boats on Florida's waterways. There probably will not be any manatees.

New state laws limit the number of new boats that can be introduced into the rivers. Speed zones are posted along all channels. And some areas are completely prohibited to boats. State income tax forms allow people to donate to a "Save the Manatee" fund. But all these measures may not be enough to save the animal.

Randy Lewis from the Florida Department of Natural Resources has noted, "The manatee is like the canary in the coal mine. If manatees can't survive in the water, you and I can't either."

The future habitat of the manatee may be limited to marine parks such as this one in Florida if people don't change their destructive environmental habits now.

Chapter 6

Why Does It Matter?

MOST OF US RECOGNIZE that it is important to save Earth's natural wealth—the resources of our planet. But some of us don't realize that the great variety of living things are part of that natural wealth. That great variety—variety within a species, variety among species, and variety in the habitats where species live—is called biodiversity.

Each plant and animal fills a different niche (or "spot") within an ecosystem. Different species have developed to fill specific niches over millions of years, and many people feel that living things have a fundamental right to continue filling those niches.

John Muir, the "father of forest conservation" in the United States, did not ask what usefulness a specific plant or animal might have. He insisted that each one was worth saving just because it was there.

FACT

Muir's idea has been called the "visionary" or "philosophical" approach to wildlife preservation. Other people take a more practical, or pragmatic, view. Or, as naturalist Aldo Leopold put it: "The first law of intelligent tinkering is to save all the pieces."

The Practical View

Every plant and animal lives as part of a whole habitat. Without all parts of the habitat working together, none of the parts—plants and animals—can continue to flourish.

Humans are also part of that picture. The existence of

The limited distribution of the *Arizona hedgehog cactus* makes it vulnerable to illegal collecting, mining, off-road recreational vehicles, and road construction.

Arizona

Historic Range Present Range

some of the species affects us very directly. Perhaps they provide fiber, or medicine, or food. Some of them affect us more indirectly. We could find a substitute for earthworms used in fishing, for example, but we could not do without the aerating and stirring of the soil that earthworms do. We depend on good soil for food.

It is reasonable to take a human-centered view of why we should protect other species. Our body processes—both chemical and physical—are basically the same as other animals, and even, to some degree, the same as plants. The things we do that hurt other species, we also do—in the long run—to ourselves. If we can learn how to protect other species, we will also be protecting ourselves. If we can understand the stresses of a closed-in habitat, if we can appreciate the deaths that pollution causes, surely we can begin to realize that by protecting the Earth's environment we are protecting ourselves.

Environmental Monitors. Some species are referred to as environmental monitors. They are so sensitive to changes in the environment that the health of their population indicates the health of their habitat, and thus the health of our own environment.

For example, when birds of prey such as peregrine fal-

cons and bald eagles began to decline rapidly, something was clearly very wrong in the environment. Scientists found that the pesticide DDT, which had been used liberally for many years, was destroying the reproductive abilities of these species. The use of DDT in the United States was quickly outlawed, and naturalists have been working ever since to rebuild populations of these birds.

Chemicals that are so poisonous to birds can't help but have a bad effect on the environment, including humans.

Effects on Habitats. We don't know enough yet to understand the functions that all of the different animals and plants serve in nature, so we have to preserve all we can—just in case. For example, officials decided to remove Nile crocodiles from an African lake, assuming that such a move would increase the number of fish available for people to eat. Instead, the edible fish numbers began to decline. Why?

The bald eagle, like the peregrine falcon, was threatened by DDT in its food sources. The eagle eggshells were so thin that they often broke before the eaglets hatched (left). But because the eagle is a national symbol, a lot of money and effort was channeled into its preservation and it has rebounded quite well (right).

Nature's ecosystems are perfectly balanced until humans interfere. When sea otters became extinct in Canadian waters, their main food, sea urchins, multiplied and destroyed the plant growth.

Because trash fish—the ones that weren't edible—were stronger than food fish. With no crocodiles to eat the trash fish, they quickly overwhelmed the food fish. Similarly, the results of letting a species or a population become extinct cannot be predicted.

The playful sea otter became extinct in Canadian waters in 1929. The numbers of sea urchins, among otters' favorite food, began to multiply. Sea urchins graze among seaweed forests on the ocean floor. Their growing numbers devastated the plant growth around Vancouver Island. Without plants, fish and other sea creatures lacked hiding places and food, and their numbers decreased.

Nearly 100 otters were released in the area between 1969 and 1972. Almost immediately, the sea urchin count began to go down, and a balanced ocean habitat began to develop.

Usefulness to Humans. We have no way of knowing in advance whether a species might ultimately have some direct use for humans. The leathery shrub called jojoba was regarded as just another plant until it was found to contain an oil that is as fine in quality as the oil of the sperm whale. Today, jojoba is used widely in industry and cosmetics.

Another shrub called the guayule contains high amounts of natural rubber. Synthetic rubber is made from petroleum that has to be pumped from the Earth, damaging more wildlife. The fact that rubber can be grown in desert country is particularly appealing.

So why save species? It's just plain safer. We never know when we might need them.

Arguments Against

The Endangered Species Act must be renewed by Congress in late 1992. In preparation for the growing body of arguments for and against renewal, the St. Louis *Post-Dispatch* in October 1991 published an editorial saying: "We should abandon the Endangered Species Act. It isn't working. By trying to save everything, we end up saving nothing. We should cut our losses."

No one can prove whether the act has actually rescued a species or not. Would the California condor be gone already if the act had not existed? No one knows for sure. However, the USFWS says that there are currently about 60 species with numbers increasing or range expanding. This would probably not be the case if the act did not exist.

To many people, however, that doesn't matter. What matters is that the need to save a species sometimes comes in sharp conflict with human needs—with people and their jobs.

Preventing Development. Some people insist that economic development has suffered in the face of the need to protect a plant or animal. That statement has been made more often since the northern spotted owl was put on the endangered list, thus protecting the old-growth forests of northern California and Oregon

The *eastern indigo snake* needs mature pine forests to live in. Deforestation for cropland and for lumber is destroying its habitat.

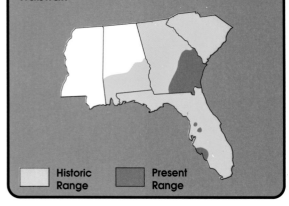

Historic Range   Present Range

The *Indiana bat* migrates from its summer woodland habitat to breed in limestone caves. About 85% hibernate in 7 caves in the Midwest. By 1991 less than 200,000 remained. Human disturbance during hibernation is the major cause for their decline.

Hibernation Caves

where the owl lives. Angry citizens of the Northwest have implied that thousands of loggers lost their jobs because of one little owl. See page 90.

The Cost. Is it worth the money? Some people have claimed that billions of dollars have been spent to save a few animals. But in reality probably not more than about $335 million had been spent through 1991 by the USFWS since the ESA began. That's less than the cost of one bomber, less than fixing a few federal highways, less than is spent to protect animals for hunting. If the act has failed, it's because the USFWS's budget has been cut year after year when more money was needed to do the job.

Because we don't know exactly how many species have become extinct in recent years or how many are in real danger today, some people think that the problem must not be as bad as is often stated. If it were really bad, they think, the scientists would *know*. But if we have to wait until we have research and data on everything, it will be too late.

Some scientists have projected into the next century a loss of 40,000 species per year. We just don't know enough about the natural world and all its interweavings to predict the effect of losing such incredible numbers of species.

Our understanding of the relationship of plant and animal life to the environment is very incomplete. But we do know that harming the Earth's environment and depleting its resources will result in a loss of its beauty and its ability to sustain life as we now know it.

It's possible that the loss of a single species could start a chain reaction that, in the long run, will affect many other species. It has been estimated, for example, that if a plant becomes extinct, it can eventually take with it up to 30 other species, including insects, higher animals, and even other plants.

FACT

Our lives depend on the biodiversity of our planet. Les Kaufman of the New England Aquarium says, "We are part of a common fabric of life. Our survival is dependent on the integrity of the fabric, for the loss of a few critical threads could lead to a quick unraveling of the whole."

Spotted Owls, Old Trees & Cancer

There are no specific rules protecting ecosystems in the Endangered Species Act. The Forest Service is required to "provide for diversity of plant and animal communities," but that is a very vague order. However, the Service is also supposed to identify those species that serve as monitors of the forest's environmental health. The northern spotted owl is such a monitor in the old-growth forests of the Northwest.

Under the act, one of the best ways to protect an entire ecosystem is to have it declared a critical habitat for a species. Conservationists then protect both the ecosystem and any threatened species that live in it.

The old forests of the Pacific Northwest contain huge hemlocks, Douglas firs, and cedars that form a mass of greenery on top (the canopy). These are at least 200 years old and some are as much as 400 years old. Within the forest ecosystem, dying trees are one kind of habitat. Fallen trees rotting on the ground are another. The canopy itself is another. And there are many more. Thousands of plant and animal species make up the various habitats.

Many logging companies use selective cutting, which is visible in the background of this photo—they don't take all the trees at once. But much of the forest is still destroyed although not as completely as a clear-cut area, shown in the foreground.

The forest once covered most of the northwestern states from San Francisco, California, on up into Canada. But only 5 or 6 percent of the forestland remains. The trees have all been cut, usually by clear-cutting, which means that the entire forest—shrubs, new growth, and all—is cut down at one time. Clear-cutting destroys all the habitats, leaving nothing but ruin in its place. The wasted, degraded land left after clear-cutting is of no use to the spotted owl, although the barred owl can move into it. Of the old-growth forest that remains to the spotted owl, 96 percent is in national forest. It can be protected if enough people insist.

The northern spotted owl lives under the canopy of the

Among the habitats destroyed by clear-cutting is that of the northern spotted owl. In order to survive, pairs of such owls need plenty of forest in which to roam in their search for food.

ancient trees. About 16 inches (40 centimeters) long, with a wingspan of 42 inches (1.1 meters), it has no ear tufts, unlike many owls. The owl nests in the holes that form in old trees. It eats squirrels, but it ranges over hundreds of miles to find them. During warm weather it stays near the ground where it's cool. Cold weather sends it up into the forest canopy where it can be warmed by the sun.

In 1986 a panel of bird experts recommended that a population of 1,500 breeding pairs—which mate for life—be preserved and that each pair should have at least 2,500 acres (1,000 hectares) of forest. In addition, they said that the chunks of forest separated by clear-cut areas were not adequate; they should be connected by large corridors of forest. Even the Forest Service admitted that the plan they created in response to the recommendations had no more than a moderate chance of saving the owl.

In early 1988, the Fish and Wildlife Service refused to list the spotted owl as threatened. The Sierra Club Legal Defense Fund took the USFWS to court. Logging was stopped on federal lands until a decision was made. A federal judge ruled in November that the USFWS had acted "contrary to law." The Forest Service set up a committee to develop a plan to save the owl. The committee recommended that 3 million acres (1.2 million hectares) of ancient forest in several large sections be left uncut for the owls.

But the committee was practical, too. Knowing that they could not shut off all the forest to loggers, they wrote: "To ignore the human condition in conservation strategies is to fail." The plan called for areas between owl sections to be logged selectively, instead of clear-cut, so that forest canopy would be left to the spotted owls flying between sections.

Otherwise, they would themselves become prey to the larger great horned owl, which hunts in the open.

In June 1990, the Fish and Wildlife Service agreed to list the northern spotted owl as threatened. Immediately, major news stories came out saying that as many as 28,000 loggers and related workers were going to lose their jobs during the coming years. Entire towns exist only because of logging.

E, The Environmental Magazine, described the situation as follows: "Pacific Northwest loggers look at the northern spotted owl and see their next great depression. Environmentalists look at this rare creature and see the last of our ancient forests about to be lost to human greed. The media look at 'owls versus jobs' and see an emotional civil war without end."

In May 1992, after many months of protest, the Endangered Species Committee (the "God squad") voted to allow immediate logging on 1,700 acres (680 hectares) of spotted owl forest in Oregon. They also recommended that Congress pass a law opening half of the old-growth forest to logging in order to preserve jobs in the timber industry.

Interior Secretary Manuel Lujan called the recommendation a "preservation" plan instead of a "recovery" plan for the owl. Most environmentalists, however, call the plan a disaster for both the northern spotted owls and the old-growth forest. They are concerned that the decision means there is little hope for renewal of a strong Endangered Species Act. They know that many species will live or die by the decisions soon to be made.

The yew tree is found in the old-growth forests of the Pacific Northwest. Recent research has detected a chemical in the yew bark that may be valuable in fighting cancer. Fortunately, researchers have found the chemical in other materials, but if old-growth forests continue to be harvested, how many other valuable species will be in danger?

Chapter 7

Are There Solutions?

IS IT REALLY POSSIBLE TO STOP the extinction of plant and animal species on Earth? Most naturalists regretfully think it is probably not possible . . . not without a major change in people's thinking. Human beings made the conditions that are extinguishing the planet's biodiversity, and most humans are unwilling—or unable—to make the necessary changes in their life-styles to prevent further loss of species. In addition, the human population is continuing to grow so rapidly that there is neither the time nor the room to rescue more than a few species.

Fortunately, we can take steps that will limit the loss.

Keeping Track of Species

One of the main requirements for protecting species is information. It isn't enough for an official or developer to look at a tract of land and just think, "Yes, it has grass, trees, insects, birds, weeds, and bushes." Instead, he or she must know that the area contains a small wetland where migrating birds stop, that a species of small flowering plants is one population of only three or four left in the wild, and so on.

Every area has its wildlife experts, people who have lived with and tramped the region for so long that they know everything that lives there. All over the world, those experts are putting what they know into an information pool called a computer database.

The Nature Conservancy has created the Natural Heritage Program and Conservation Data Center Network—a huge inventory of rare and endangered plants and animals. Often called the Heritage Network, the system includes 82 biodiversity data centers in North and South America. The

centers are usually run by a state natural resources department or other agency. Other countries are working on developing heritage networks of their own, which will link with the American system. The ultimate goal is a computerized inventory of all the world's wildlife.

The database is used when a new project is getting started. It might help determine if a new road would threaten an important habitat, or if draining a wetland might destroy a threatened species. The information includes where a species is found, how rare it is, what it eats, who owns the various places where it is found, the names of the scientists who are experts on the species, and so on.

A special project of the Heritage Networks of New Jersey, Maryland, and Delaware has been the sighting and recording of songbirds flying south along the Atlantic Coast. When the information is put into the computer, they hope to be able to discover the main songbird habitats and check them to see which ones might need protecting. Through the network centers in Latin America, they hope to be able to identify the winter quarters of migrating songbirds and keep them from falling to the ax. It doesn't do any good to protect the northern sites if the southern ones disappear.

Making A Nature Database

You can create an information database of the wildlife in your area. If you have access to a computer, use it. Otherwise, you can keep the information in a card file or notebook.

Write to the Department of Natural Resources in your state or province to learn which species are endangered. Doing library research and talking to the birdwatchers and other naturalists in your area, learn all you can about each species. Record any stories you learn about where the species were located in the past. Prepare maps showing where the various endangered species still live. As you walk around the area, hunt for habitats that have been damaged.

If you involve your class in the project, it will be easier to collect all the information. Work with organizations in your area to help preserve the endangered species.

Fencing Them In

There has long been a temptation to solve the problem of an endangered species, especially an animal species, by placing the animal in a zoo or a botanical garden. Put a fence around it and it will be safe, many people think.

Even when it became clear that it was better to preserve a species' habitat than to try to rescue the species itself, our solution has still been to build a fence around the known habitat and hope that the species will survive. Refuges and

97

The *African black rhinoceros* population was about 650,000 in 1968. Illegally killed for its valuable horn, fewer than 3,500 remain and those are in preserves.

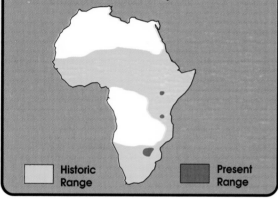

Historic Range

Present Range

preserves and national parks were developed in part on just this idea.

Today, about 90 million acres (36 million hectares) of wildlife habitat are under the protection of the National Wildlife Refuge System. The system was started by President Theodore Roosevelt in 1903 when he made Pelican Island in Florida a refuge to protect the birds that were being destroyed for their beautiful feathers. Now there are more than 400 refuges, whose primary purpose is to maintain or increase wildlife populations. Only recreational activities that involve nature are permitted.

Unlike wildlife refuges, national parks in the United States are more oriented toward people and thus are not good places for preserving species. A 1987 study showed that since the 14 national parks in the West were established, 42 species of mammals in those parks have died out. The pressures exerted by visitors, logging, and mining in national parks are so great that the parks don't make good refuges for endangered species.

On a smaller level, numerous governments and developers have left "islands" of natural habitats dotted among farms and pavement. Even islands of tropical rain forest have been left as the jungle was deforested.

But now naturalists are discovering that these habitat

Well-designed housing developments have large green "islands" that form corridors of undisturbed habitat through which animals can move.

"islands" often aren't benefiting anyone, except perhaps other animals from outside the islands. For example, songbirds that nest within a habitat island often lose their eggs to raccoons that live on the fringes of the preserve. Chemicals blow in on the wind from neighboring farms. And most important, if animals are cut off from other populations, the diversity of genes available to the breeding population becomes limited. (Or, as one writer put it, the gene pool becomes a gene puddle.) The animals become too inbred, which can be destructive to the species.

Some animals need more room to roam than is available in preserves, or even in the largest national park. A panther, for example, may cover 20 miles (32 kilometers) in a night hunting for food. Its total territory may cover 150 square miles (388 square kilometers).

A new branch of biology called conservation biology is concerned with studying these problems. Conservation biologists are using a computer modeling system called Population Viability Analysis to predict the likelihood that a specific population of animals can survive if it is cut off from others of its species.

Helping the Housing Shortage

You can help keep birds off the endangered list by providing houses where they can nest and raise their young. When nesting sites are scarce, many birds will inhabit constructed birdhouses.

Use unpainted, seasoned wood. Birds are not attracted to bright colors or the smell of paint and varnish. Be sure the joints are tightly nailed or screwed together to keep out the rain. Do not put a perch on the house. Nesting birds don't need one. Hinge one side of the roof for easy cleaning. In late fall, remove the old nesting material and debris for the next spring's occupants.

Decide which kind of bird you hope to attract and decide where you will put the birdhouse. The drawings give some suggestions, but you might want to visit a nearby nature preserve or bird sanctuary for more ideas.

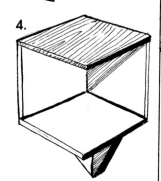

Bird	Height from Ground	Diameter of Hole
1. chickadee	10 ft. (3.0 m) on post or tree	1⅛ in. (2.9 cm)
2. titmouse	12 ft. (3.7 m) in tree	1¼ in. (3.2 cm)
3. nuthatch	15 ft. (4.6 m) on tree	1¼ in. (3.2 cm)
4. robin	low bush or tree	open box on its side
5. wren	10 ft. (3.0 m) on post or tree	⅞ in. (2.3 cm)
6. screech owl	15 ft. (4.6 m) in tree	3¼ in. (8.2 cm) hollow log
7. tree swallow	10 ft. (3.0 m) in tree	1½ in. (3.8 cm)
8. bluebird	8 ft. (2.4 m) on post	1½ in. (3.8 cm)

Corridors. Many populations isolated by concrete and development can't survive. Since the mid-1980s, many conservation biologists have suggested that a park or reserve must be attached to another by a corridor of wilderness—a *conservation corridor*.

In planning corridors and refuges, naturalists concentrate on the largest and widest roaming species, such as bears and wolves. This isn't done because bears and wolves are necessarily the most important, but because protection of large habitats guarantees the protection of smaller habitats for other animals that are located within the larger area.

A conservation corridor may be just a brush-covered riverbank. It might be an abandoned railroad track that has been turned into a hiking trail. Whatever, it must supply the animals with cover to get from one wilderness area to another.

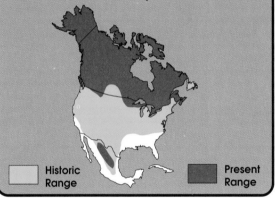

The *gray wolf* has been extinct in northern Eurasian regions (except Siberia, Russia) for years. In the United States the wolves were exterminated to protect livestock.

Historic Range

Present Range

The Netherlands is proposing to build 750 tunnels under the many highways in that small country to give badgers, martens, and red deer a way to get safely through the traffic. It may also build a number of overhead crossings for those animals that won't go underground.

FACT

Wilderness Study Areas. The United States government, through the Bureau of Land Management, has turned pockets of habitat into wilderness study areas (WSAs). Wilderness study areas vary from 1,000 acres (400 hectares) for a special secluded beach to a small mountain range. They are chosen to give people opportunities to be alone, to indulge in hiking or other gentle recreation, to explore historic or environmental resources, or just to enjoy nature.

In 1991, the government recommended that an additional 2.3 million acres (944,000 hectares) be added to California's WSA system, making a total of more than 8 million acres (3 million hectares) in that one state alone.

But Will They Do Any Good? In the long run, even protection of habitat may not work, especially if it is in relatively small pockets surrounded by normal development.

David Ehrenfeld of Rutgers University tells of the university's 60-acre (24-hectare) Hutcheson Forest, which has never been cut or plowed and can be visited only by special ecologically-minded visitors. Even so, the forest has gradually been taken over by alien species and harmed by chemicals brought on the wind.

Alaska's Kenai Moose Range, a wildlife refuge, isn't safe from oil pollution. Pressure is being exerted on governments to allow oil exploration and drilling in wilderness areas—areas vital to permanent and migratory wildlife.

"You can fence out people, but you cannot fence out their effects," Ehrenfeld says. "Alien introduced pests, acid rain, ozone, insecticide residues, drifting herbicide, heavy metals, atmospheric particulates—these effects and creations of our society can be anywhere and everywhere on Earth."

Captive Breeding

Sometimes the last hope of a species is for the few remaining plants or animals to be taken into captivity and helped in every way possible to keep new generations going. The hope is that a species that now exists only in captivity may someday be returned to the wild.

Many naturalists think that captive breeding in zoos may turn out to be the last refuge for what have been called the "charismatic megavertebrates"—the large species that people find particularly fascinating, such as elephants, rhinos, gorillas, and even the huge vultures called condors.

Captive breeding consists of capturing all or nearly all of the few remaining wild creatures of a species, caging them, and trying to hand-raise the young. It is hoped that someday there will be enough animals to take some back to the wild.

The American Association of Zoological Parks and Aquariums has a Species Survival Plan that oversees captive breeding programs. Rarely is the work done at just one zoo, because if some catastrophe happened there, the species would be gone. So the work must be coordinated among various zoos and aquariums that are holding the animals, so that the greatest diversity of genes is preserved. Assisting in that program is a computer database called the International Species Identification System, which is abbreviated ISIS. Isis was the Egyptian god of fertility.

One of the most publicized and successful of the captive breeding programs in North America has been the international effort to bring the huge whooping crane back from virtual extinction. See the end of this chapter.

A Glance at Successful Programs. One of the earliest animals to be captured in the wild and put into a captive breeding program was the Arabian oryx. This white antelope of the Middle East had been hunted to extinction. In the early 1960s when several world organizations decided to try to rescue it, they were able to find only three animals in the wild. Six others lived in zoos. Those nine animals had to serve as the entire stock for breeding the oryx back into reasonable numbers.

The few remaining oryx were sent to the Maytag Zoo in Phoenix, Arizona, where they were bred successfully. Some were moved to San Diego Wild Animal Park to avoid the possibility of catastrophe.

In the early 1980s, a small herd from the San Diego group was taken to the deserts of Oman. They first spent a year in a huge enclosure in the desert and then were released. Nearby feeding troughs were moved every few days farther and farther from the enclosure to entice them out into the wilderness. The herd is succeeding in the wild. They are breeding and raising young. And more animals are being released regularly, with plans to release at least 300 altogether.

The little monkey called the golden lion tamarin was having trouble reproducing in its shrinking

Some captive breeding programs have been quite successful. The National Zoo and the World Wildlife Fund worked together to rescue the golden lion tamarin. Ninety of these monkeys were returned to the wild in 1991.

rainforest habitat in Brazil. The National Zoo in Washington, D.C., working with the World Wildlife Fund, found solutions for the reproductive problems and began to return tamarins to the wild. If the rain forest itself survives, perhaps the tamarins will, too.

The American red wolf, which was within a few animals of extinction, has successfully been bred and introduced into a wildlife refuge in North Carolina and finally into Great Smoky Mountains National Park. Naturalists are excited about the success because they would like to try reintroducing the gray wolf into Yellowstone National Park. Many ranchers in nearby areas object, however, because they are afraid that the wolves will go after their livestock.

The little black-footed ferret disappeared when its habitat—prairie dog towns—was systematically poisoned to get rid of the prairie dogs. The ferret was already thought to be extinct when, in 1981, a small colony was discovered living in a prairie dog town in Wyoming. When that colony appeared to be heading toward extinction, several of the animals were caught to start a breeding program. In 1991, the small animals were being reintroduced into the wild.

At the time of the Lewis and Clark Expedition in the early 1800s, California condors were visible up and down

The American red wolf (left) and the black-footed ferret (right) have been reintroduced into the wild through captive breeding programs. But the same human enemies remain—ranchers and farmers worried about their livestock.

105

To ensure that a baby condor doesn't begin to think that it's human, a puppet that looks like an adult condor is used to feed the young bird. Studies have shown that condors have a better chance of surviving in the wild if human contact is slight.

A California condor grows to maturity in its hacksite. When it is ready for return to the wild, the net is removed and the bird flies away.

the entire West Coast. When the Condor Research Center was founded in 1980 as a joint effort of the National Audubon Society and USFWS, there were probably no more than 20 of these vultures with the 10-foot (3-meter) wingspan left. After the winter of 1985, only one breeding pair of birds remained. Several adults were found to have died of lead poisoning due to eating animals that had been shot.

After much debate, the Fish and Wildlife Service decided to capture the six remaining birds, hoping to breed them. The first chick to survive the new regime hatched in 1988. Several dozen have been raised since then.

Also in 1988, several closely related Andean condors were released in the Los Padres Mountains near Los Angeles. The birds were all females so that they could not start breeding and take up permanent residence in California. The behavior, eating habits, and territory of the released birds were studied in detail so that the information could be used in helping the California condor return to the wild.

The first attempt to return a California condor to the wild was made when a young bird was released in January 1992. Time will tell if a major captive breeding program will work for these amazing birds.

Problems with Captive Breeding. Many naturalists do not like the idea of captive breeding. First, they fear that if enough people come to think that captive breeding answers the problem of endangered species, they will avoid dealing with the more complicated task of preserving natural ecosystems.

When Florida was given permission to start capturing young Florida panthers for captive breeding, for example, an animal rights group called Fund for Animals went to court to get the process stopped.

D. J. Schubert of the Fund says, "I think that captive breeding in this case is a Band-Aid for covering up an oozing, festering wound, which is the habitat issue. It's an easy way out. We can use all our technology to deal with these panthers in a zoo rather than dealing with hard issues about habitat destruction—cattle grazing, urban development, and the citrus industry. After we breed these animals in captivity—if we ever can—where are they going to go?"

A compromise was reached in court, allowing the state to capture six Florida panther kittens on condition that the real habitat problems be confronted.

Second, the programs can be very expensive. The California condor program alone costs $750,000 annually. Because millions of dollars are spent to return a few animals to the wild, the temptation will be to breed only those species that are romantic or fascinating—especially mammals and birds. The less interesting animals will not get adequate funding to rescue them. There is also a philosophical question of whether money should be spent to breed animals that no longer exist in the wild.

Third, animals that spend a lot of time in cages may lose their fear of humans, which would put them in danger if they were returned to the wild. Also, genetic changes can occur in captivity that can affect the ability of the returned animals to survive.

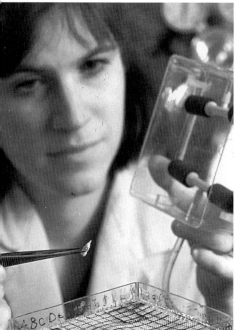

Seed banks located around the world store seeds of many plants, but the programs concentrate on food-producing plants. There is probably neither the time nor the money to collect, identify, and store every known plant on the chance that it may someday be wiped out in the wild.

Fourth, if a habitat was so degraded that the animals needed to be taken captive, there is little likelihood that any habitat appropriate for the animals will ever be found.

Fifth, population experts predict that it may take between 150 and 200 years for Earth's growing human population to stabilize (stop growing) and even start decreasing. Naturalists involved in captive breeding programs forecast that it will be necessary to continue to breed animals in captivity until that stage of stability is reached. Only then will it actually be possible to analyze the condition of the various species of the planet.

Regional Planning

A plan to rescue the slow-moving, foot-long desert tortoise is one of several regional habitat plans that take into account all the major uses of a region in trying to protect a species and its habitat.

Two-thirds of the population of Nevada live in Clark County, which surrounds the city of Las Vegas, and perhaps 5,000 people are moving to the area every month. Also within that same area of the Mojave Desert live at least 50 endangered species, including the desert tortoise. About 1 foot (30 centimeters) long, the desert tortoise thrives in the hot, arid desert by burrowing into the ground, but it has not shunned life within the city limits of Las Vegas.

In 1989, scientists found that perhaps half the once-thriving desert tortoise population of about 100,000 had died from a combination of vandals shooting at them and pressures that included cattle grazing, housing development,

108

and off-road vehicles. In addition, the animals had acquired a mysterious respiratory disease. Another pressure came from another animal. Human population growth had brought the raven, which readily feeds on garbage dumps, into the area in large numbers. Ravens consume baby tortoises as readily as rancid beef from the garbage. An additional major problem for the desert tortoise has been the famed annual Barstow-to-Vegas Motorcycle Race. Vehicles racing across the fragile desert floor have torn up many acres of tortoise habitat.

The species was given an emergency listing under the Endangered Species Act in 1989 and a permanent threatened listing in 1990. That meant that if a single animal was seen on the site of a new housing development, heavy machinery had to stop its work. Only projects that had been started before the ruling was made were allowed to continue.

Unable to wait for complete habitat plans to be worked out—a process that might take three years—developers agreed to pay $550 per acre (0.4 hectare) into a fund used to acquire desert habitat away from the city. At least 100,000 acres (40,500 hectares) were purchased in the first year, with plans to acquire an additional 300,000 acres (121,000 hectares) by the end of 1995. Within the set-aside area, grazing would no longer be permitted unless long-term research

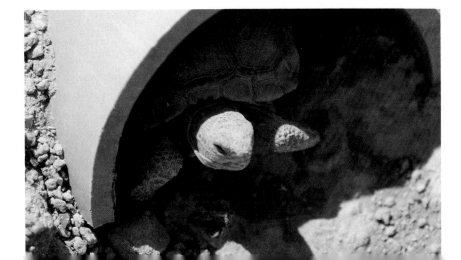

A desert tortoise at the Desert Tortoise Conservation Center outside Las Vegas, Nevada, lives in a man-made cement burrow. A compromise with developers "saved" the tortoise from extinction.

109

showed that it would be safe. Though it has taken several court cases, the motorcycle race has been canceled.

When tortoises are found in areas being developed, they are collected and moved to the new 222-acre (90-hectare) Desert Tortoise Conservation Center. From there, the tortoises can be studied in research projects, sent to zoos, used in education, or adopted by private families.

Even more significant, however, is the regional habitat approach, which integrates plans for the endangered species with developments for people. Such regional planning is also being tried in California to create habitats for a threatened lizard species and a variety of the kangaroo rat.

Tourists May Help

Oddly enough, though people going into wild areas seem to be the cause of problems with some endangered species, tourism is an important economic benefit and may guarantee that some species will survive. If the animals that attract tourists to an area are allowed to die out, the benefit will disappear.

On the island of Komodo, for example, the world-famous monitor lizard called the Komodo dragon is now down to probably less than 300 breeding females. Komodo dragons may be 10 feet (3 meters) long and weigh up to 300 pounds (136 kilograms). They have been known to eat humans, because they will eat anything that moves, including the young of their species. Often the only thing that protects a young one is its ability to climb trees, a skill the adults lose.

A larger animal, even a human, can be killed simply by the bite of a Komodo dragon. Its saliva contains poisons that kill whatever it has bitten even if the prey gets away. Then the dragon just has to go and fetch the prey after it dies. The dragon's digestive juices are powerful enough to digest bones and all.

Nowadays the Komodo dragons don't even need to hunt—they are given food so that tourists can watch them eat. The entire island of Komodo is a national park. The nation of Indonesia keeps the animals in good condition and their numbers strong because tourists bring money to the islands.

There have probably never been many Komodo dragons, so though their numbers may seem endangered, there is probably sufficient dragon population for them to keep going.

The Komodo dragon was almost extinct because it was captured for collectors. Indonesia saved the lizard by making Komodo Island a national park. Tourists bring in money the country needs.

Tourist-supported rescue will not work for some animals, however. Many endangered species will not breed if there's too much human activity in their vicinity. These are the animals that will probably become extinct.

One of the most vulnerable types of areas that can fall victim to visitors is the coral reef. Snorkelers, boat anchors and boat waste, pollution—all these impact severely on fragile coral reefs that took thousands of years to build. They can be destroyed in a tiny percentage of that time, taking with them the many marine species that depend on the reefs for habitat.

Getting Our Act Together

It's interesting to read stories of individual species that are being rescued and how the rescuing is being done. But there are even more stories of species that are becoming extinct without anyone taking notice.

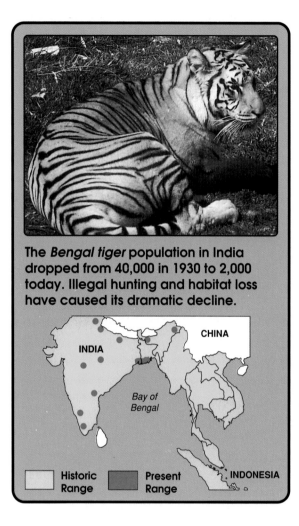

The *Bengal tiger* population in India dropped from 40,000 in 1930 to 2,000 today. Illegal hunting and habitat loss have caused its dramatic decline.

In the long run, saving a single species, a habitat and all its occupants, or even whole ecosystems, is going to require more than last-ditch efforts. A species on the brink of extinction or a habitat about to be attacked by bulldozers can only be treated as an emergency. There is not enough time for detailed studies.

The human population of the Earth is not going to get smaller any time soon. We are going to need more places to live, more agricultural land, and more recreational areas. We can probably have those things and preserve natural habitat, too, if planning is done in advance. Cities can be more densely populated and more compact. Suburbs can have habitat islands and conservation corridors through which animals can move. Countryside can be preserved if chemicals and other pollutants are kept under control.

None of these things will happen unless individuals care for the Earth. Cities, counties, states, and nations need to begin regional planning that will limit the outward growth of populated areas and give wildlife the territory it needs.

Bill Reffalt of the Wilderness Society says, "The Endangered Species Act is a safety net for species we've put in jeopardy while we get our act together to take care of the planet." It's time to get our act together.

The Whooping Crane

The tallest and one of the most elegant birds in North America is the whooping crane. It stands 5 feet (1.5 meters) tall and has a wingspread of more than 6 feet (1.8 meters). Its beautiful white body rests on thin black legs, and the top of its head is featherless, with red skin. Whooping cranes do beautiful mating dances unlike those of any other birds.

Unfortunately, these wonderful birds have long been the target of hunters. In addition, many of the prairie wetland areas in which they rest and breed have been destroyed. In 1870 there were probably no more than 600 cranes. By 1940, the number was down to an alarming 16.

Traditionally, the birds nested all over the upper Midwest. Now they are limited primarily to the Wood Buffalo National Park in remote northern Canada, which was established in 1922 to protect the wood bison. The whooping cranes spend the winter on the Texas Gulf Coast at Aransas National Wildlife Refuge. Between those two sites, the birds need 2,600 miles (4,180 kilometers) of flyway.

The Aransas Refuge had barely been established in 1937 when the whooping crane count was found to be so alarmingly low. Year by year, the flock was watched. Additional refuges were established along the flyways, so

113

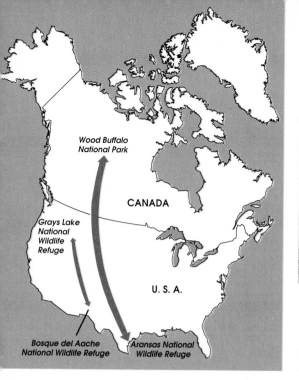

Whooping cranes lay their eggs in wetland habitat at Wood Buffalo National Park, Canada, and at Grays Lake National Wildlife Refuge, Idaho. One group winters as far as 2,600 miles (4,180 kilometers) south at Aransas National Wildlife Refuge, Texas.

that the birds would have safe areas to land.

Then, in 1967, the Audubon Society, Canadian Wildlife Service, and USFWS began a program of captive breeding. Because whooping cranes lay two eggs and usually only one matures, naturalists were able to filch one egg from every nest they could find. Between 1967 and 1974, eggs laid in the wild were taken from nests in Wood Buffalo National Park to the Patuxent Research Center in Laurel, Maryland. There the eggs were carefully hatched and the chicks were reared by hand.

It has been a slow process because the birds do not mate until they are at least five years old. Also, disease has some-times struck without warning, killing some of the captive birds. Less than half of all the eggs taken into captivity produced young that survived to grow up. But by 1985, the flock at Patuxent numbered 38 birds. When the flock was endangered by a disease in 1989, some of the birds were sent to the International Crane Foundation in Baraboo, Wisconsin, where more cranes are being bred.

A separate flock was established beginning in 1974 in Grays Lake National Wildlife Refuge in Idaho by placing whooping crane eggs in the nests of smaller sandhill cranes. The sandhills were willing to act as foster parents to the large creatures that appeared in their nests. This group travels only about 750 miles (1,200 kilometers) to winter quarters near Albuquerque, New Mexico.

At any time, one of these small flocks could be endangered further. For example, in 1989, when an oil spill happened in the Gulf of Mexico, oil almost reached the Aransas Refuge. Some locations on the crane migration routes are known to have a disease called avian cholera. Members of the National Audubon Society actively help take care of the cranes by preventing them from landing in such areas and by keeping track of their migration paths twice a year. Migrating birds are particularly vulnerable to colliding with power-lines.

The prospects for the whooping crane are good. The possibility of developing another flock that would live in Florida is being discussed. Two nations and many volunteers are tending to the future of the whooping cranes, both in the wild and in captivity.

A newly hatched whooper chick bred in captivity is often very susceptible to disease. However, enough have survived to give biologists hope for the species' long-term survival.

Chapter 8

Taking Action

HUMANS HAVE CAUSED MOST of the problems that endanger the planet's wildlife. And humans can solve most of those problems if they have the will. Fortunately, individuals who act out of their own concern can have a profound effect on the fate of many endangered species. You can help, too.

Resolve to buy nothing that comes from an endangered, threatened, or rare animal. These include items made of ivory and turtle shell, as well as body parts. That sounds pretty gruesome, but some people like bear paws and gall bladders. Gorilla heads bring poachers a great deal of money.

Pay Attention to Life Around You

Endangered and threatened species are not just plants and animals in distant places. Populations of specific species can be threatened in your own area. Be aware that the land around you is not just land, it's habitat. Something lives there, and it may be a rare something.

Get to know what plant and animal species are endangered in your area. You can obtain a list in your school or public library, or write the state natural resources or conservation department.

As development takes place around you, make sure that a new parking lot, road, or subdivision will not destroy the habitat of plants or animals that might be in trouble. Work with your town or county officials to come up with alternative sites if a plan affects endangered or threatened species.

Evaluate your own outdoor recreational activities. If you like hiking and collecting wildflowers, know what is legal to collect in your area. If you like power-boating and jet skiing, make absolutely certain that you are doing these dangerous

Chemical pollution of surface water and groundwater from farm runoff has become a major problem. Many farmers are now using non-polluting natural fertilizers and pest control to grow their crops.

activities in areas where there are no endangered animals. If you go boating off Hawaii, for example, you may be entering the realm of the humpback whales or green sea turtles. In Florida rivers and canals, you might be endangering manatees.

Become acquainted with the state and national wildlife refuges in your area. Talk to their education specialists, and get to know the species that are being protected. Ask if you can help out on some of the special projects that the refuges become involved in, such as the annual bird count. Perhaps someday you could become a guide in the refuge, helping to answer other people's questions.

Enjoy your balloons on the ground. Yes, it's fun to watch balloons drift off on the wind and wonder where they will end up. But too often they end up in the stomachs of animals.

If your family farms, or owns a home, take advantage of the natural inclinations of some animals to eat pests. A number of laboratories can provide through the mail any of 250 species of bugs that will eat other, less wanted, insects. Certain ladybug beetles, for example, will willingly eat up every destructive aphid that comes near them. Such pest control is better for the environment—and cheaper—than using chemical pesticides.

If you are a hunter or fisherman, know exactly what it is legal to catch. Be completely familiar with those legal species so that you won't harm anything that is in danger or out of season. If you see people taking illegal animals, alert the authorities.

Live a Kindly Life

Anything we can do to protect the environment in general protects living things. If we take it for granted that there will always be all the water we want, we may be endangering something by our assumptions. If we assume that there will always be enough electric power, new power plants and lines may spring up. Mining coal or oil to run them could endanger habitats far away.

Recycle everything you can because trash ends up in habitat-consuming landfills. New products require minerals to be mined, power to process, and fuels to transport. All of those basic activities can affect plant and animal habitat. Be sure to buy products made with recycled materials, otherwise separating your trash does little good.

Contribute . . .

. . . **your money.** Every project to rescue a species requires a great deal of money. Contribute all you can to your favorite causes. Perhaps you and your friends can organize a fund-raising campaign to help fund a project in your area.

Encourage others to contribute to such organizations as The Nature Conservancy and the Audubon Society, which purchase habitat to protect endangered species and ecosystems. In addition, they participate in "Debt-for-Nature" programs. In these, the organization purchases some of a nation's debt from a specific bank. They pay off the debt and in return the country agrees to protect the resources and endangered species of a specific area. This is a particularly good method of working with developing countries that owe a great deal of money to industrialized nations. Such programs can stop the development of valuable land.

...your attention. One of the most important things you can do now and in coming years is to stay interested and informed. If you think it's important for the future of our planet to preserve species, act on your convictions.

The economic recession of 1991-92 brought a serious swing in public opinion. Many people began to say, "To heck with endangered species. We need jobs!" Sometimes it's not even the endangered species that is the real cause of the problem. For example, the northern spotted owl has been blamed for "taking away" jobs from loggers in the Northwest. And yet the economic problems of the logging companies started by jobs being automated and logs sold to Japan unfinished, eliminating sawmill jobs in the United States.

It is rare that we must choose between one thing (jobs) and the other (a rescued species). Usually there are ways to compromise, or there are different ways of looking at the situation. People need to remain open-minded to see them.

Encourage your state, province, or federal government to move faster on the protection of the many plants and animals that are known to be threatened but have not yet been officially put on any lists so that they get protection. There are currently almost 4,000 species in the United States waiting to be added to the list. They can't be helped until they are on the list.

The international wildlife trade is worth billions of dollars. Although the U.S. government confiscates illegal goods, such as these, smugglers all too often succeed in getting their illegal items into the country.

Unite with Others

Join environmental groups that are working to preserve and restore the land. By joining, you will become part of the effort to solve the larger problems facing our Earth—the things that one person alone can't affect too easily. But before you join, find out exactly what the group stands for and promotes, and learn what they do with any donations they receive.

Some places to write for further information are:

American Forestry Association, 1516 P. St., NW, Washington, DC 20036

Canadian Wildlife Federation, 1673 Carling Ave., Ottawa, Ontario, Canada K2A 3Z1

Center for Plant Conservation, 3115 S. Grand Blvd., St. Louis, MO 63118

Citizens for a Better Environment, 111 King St., Madison, WI 53703

Defenders of Wildlife, 1244 19th St., NW, Washington, DC 10036

Environmental Defense Fund, 1616 P St., NW, Washington, DC 20036

Friends of the Earth, 218 D St., SE, Washington, DC 20003

Fund for Animals, 200 W. 57th St., New York, NY 10019

International Crane Foundation, Shady Lane Rd., Baraboo, WI 53913-9778

National Audubon Society, 645 Pennsylvania Ave., SE, Washington, DC 20003

National Wildlife Federation, 1400 16th St., NW, Washington, DC 20036

Natural Resources Defense Council, 1350 New York Avenue, NW, #300, Washington, DC 20005

The Nature Conservancy, 1815 N. Lynn St., Arlington, VA 22209

Save the Manatee Club, 500 N. Maitland, Maitland, FL 32751

Sea Shepherd Conservation Society, P.O. Box 7000-S, Redondo Beach, CA 90277

Sierra Club, 730 Polk St., San Francisco, CA 94133

Wilderness Society, 1400 I St., NW - 10th Floor, Washington DC 20005

World Wildlife Fund, 1250 24th St., NW, Washington, DC 10027, or 90 Eglinton Ave. E., Suite 504, Toronto, Ontario, Canada M4P 2Z7

Writing Letters

Both in Canada and the United States, elected government officials are going to need to be encouraged to pass the laws and funding necessary to preserve as many species as possible. But they need to know your opinions. Take time to write and to get others to write to the people involved in making the decisions. This is especially important when the Endangered Species Act is being changed.

State and Provincial Concerns. On issues concerning state or provincial legislation or to express your opinion about actions taken by an environmental or natural resources agency, find an address at your library and write:

Your local state or provincial legislator.

The governor of your state or premier of your province.

The director of your department of natural resources or similar environmental agency.

Federal concerns. On issues concerning federal legislation or to express your opinion about actions taken by the federal government, you can write to:

Your state's two U.S. senators. Check at your local library to discover their names. Write:

> The Honorable _____
> U.S. Senate
> Washington, DC 20510

Your local congressman. Check at your local library to discover his or her name.

> The Honorable _____
> U.S. House of Representatives
> Washington, DC 20515

Your local provincial or federal Member of Parliament. Check at your local library to discover his or her name.

> The Honorable _____
> House of Commons
> Ottawa, Ontario, Canada K1A 0A6

The President of the United States. He has the power to veto, or turn down, bills approved by Congress as well as to introduce bills of his own. He also must approve what the U.S. Fish and Wildlife Service and other agencies do.

> President _____
> The White House
> 1600 Pennsylvania Avenue, NW
> Washington, DC 20501

The Prime Minister of Canada.

> The Honorable _____
> House of Commons
> Ottawa, Ontario, Canada K1A 0A6

David Ehrenfeld tells of visiting two different oases that provided homes for Papago Indians in the deserts of the Southwest. One, a bird sanctuary in Arizona, is part of the Organ Pipe Cactus National Monument. However, it has only half the number of species of birds that live at another oasis that is only 30 miles (48 kilometers) away in Mexico. The second oasis is regularly farmed by the Papago.

The legal protection supposedly offered by being part of a national monument was less effective than just living in harmony with nature. "That is when conservation becomes reality, when people who are not actively trying to be conservationists play and work in a way that is compatible with the existence of the other native species of the region."

GLOSSARY

biodiversity - variety of living species within a region, and variety of genetic types within a species.

captive breeding - the deliberate mating of individuals within a captured population of animals in order to guarantee the survival of the species and its return to the wild.

critical habitat - specific areas containing the physical and biological features necessary for the conservation of a species. Critical habitat is supposed to be designated for any endangered species.

ecosystem - the complete system in which a collection of organisms interact with each other and with the physical environment.

endangered - in immediate danger of becoming extinct or extirpated within its range.

endemic - native to and existing nowhere else.

evolution - the change within a species sometimes leading to new species, based on genetic mutation.

extinct - no longer existing anywhere.

extirpated - extinct in a specific region but existing elsewhere.

gene - a chemical pattern within a living cell that determines a characteristic in the living thing.

global warming - gradual increase in the overall temperature of the planet caused by the addition of extra heat-holding gases to the atmosphere.

habitat - the part of an ecosystem in which a specific plant or animal lives.

inbreeding - reproduction among closely related animals; may weaken the species because there is less variety in genes.

indigenous - native to, but not necessarily endemic.

introduced - brought in from another land. Introduced species often take over territory from native species.

mutation - an accidental variation in a gene that occurs during duplication within a cell. Mutations may introduce variations into a species that will play a roll in evolution of new species.

species - any group of living things that is able to or willing to breed only within its own kind. Also, according to the Endangered Species Act, any species, subspecies, or geographically separated population.

territory - the area a specific animal will defend against intrusion by other animals of the same or sometimes related species.

threatened - likely to become endangered unless conditions improve within the species' habitat.

vulnerable - at risk but not yet threatened.

INDEX

Bold numbers = illustration

PHOTO SOURCES

Dr. Gary Benson: 98
The Bishop Museum: 9
Bonneville Power Administration: 69
Richard A. Bucich: 44
California Department of Water Resources: 89
Canadian Wildlife Service/Environment Canada: 39, 114 left
Center for Plant Conservation/Paul Cox: 75
Center for Plant Conservation/Derral Herbst: 76
Photo courtesy Center for Marine Conservation: 28 bottom left
Jessie Cohen/National Zoological Society: 57 top, 104, 111
Florida Department of Natural Resources/Marine Research Institute: 80
Florida Division of Tourism: 42 left, 81
Florida Game and Freshwater Fish Commission: 20
Food & Agriculture Organization/A. Iokem: 78
Georgia Department of Natural Resources: 74, 87
J.D. Griggs/U.S. Geological Survey: 7
Carrol Henderson: 8, 21, 32, 43, 56, 67, 73, 77
Idaho Department of Natural Resources: 68, 71
Indiana Department of Natural Resources: 88
Jack Jeffrey: 13
Dave Marshall: 11
Milwaukee Public Museum: 23
Minnesota Department of Natural Resources: 16, 17
National Fish and Wildlife Forensics Laboratory: 2, 18, 57 bottom, 58
National Marine Fisheries Service: 54 top
National Oceanic & Atmospheric Administration/Marine Debris Information Office/Steven Santona: 14 left
National Oceanic & Atmospheric Administration/Sanctuaries and Reserve Division: 6
National Park Service/M. Woodbridge Williams: 64
National Park Service/Richard Frear: 82
National Park Service/Richard V. Harris: 28 top right, top left, middle
National Park Service: 42 right
Ohio Department of Natural Resources: 70
SCP/J. Beardsell: 63
SCP/R. Michaud: 61
Sea Shepherd Conservation Society: 54 bottom, 66
Secretaria de Turismo de Mexico: 46
Patrick Silva: 14 right
Southern California Edison: 85 right
Jan Straley: 96 right
U.S. Fish & Wildlife Service/Ashton Graham: 113
U.S. Fish & Wildlife Service/Bob Stevens: 60
U.S. Fish & Wildlife Service/D. Clendenen: 106 bottom
U.S. Fish & Wildlife Service/Gaylan Rathburn: 79
U.S. Fish & Wildlife Service/Gerald Ludwig: 47, 96 left
U.S. Fish & Wildlife Service/Jim Palmer: 116
U.S. Fish & Wildlife Service/Luther Goldman: 49, 97, 102
U.S. Fish & Wildlife Service/Marty Stouffer: 105 left
U.S. Fish & Wildlife Service/R.L. Herman: 26
U.S. Fish & Wildlife Service/Randy Wilk: 91 bottom
U.S. Fish & Wildlife Service/Rich Krueger: 105 right
U.S. Fish & Wildlife Service/Robert Mesta: 106 top
U.S. Fish & Wildlife Service/Rodney Krey: 85 left
U.S. Fish & Wildlife Service/Ron Singer: 112
U.S. Fish & Wildlife Service/Steve Hillebrand: 120
U.S. Fish & Wildlife Service/Sue Rutman: 84
U.S. Fish & Wildlife Service/W. French: 38
U.S. Fish & Wildlife Service: 25, 35, 36, 41, 115
USDA Forest Service: 30, 59, 90, 91 top, 94
USDA/Agricultural Research Service: 108, 118
USDI/Bureau of Land Management: 93, 109
Greg Vaughn: 86
Terri Willis: 99
Wisconsin Department of Natural Resources: 15, 51, 52, 101

ABOUT THE AUTHORS

Jean F. Blashfield and Wallace B. Black are dedicated environmentalists, writers, and publishers who are responsible for this book and the *SAVING PLANET EARTH* series. Working together, with other environmentalists, educators, and Childrens Press, they have developed 13 other books in the *SAVING PLANET EARTH* series.

This creative team was responsible for the creation of *THE YOUNG PEOPLE'S SCIENCE ENCYCLOPEDIA* and *ABOVE AND BEYOND, THE ENCYCLOPEDIA OF AVIATION AND SPACE SCIENCES*. In addition, Jean Blashfield was the editor-in-chief of *THE YOUNG STUDENTS ENCYCLOPEDIA* and is the author of more than 25 other books. Wallace Black, a former pilot in the United States Air Force, is the author of a series of books on World War II.